Working After Welfare

This book is due on the last date stamped below.
Failure to return books on the date due may result
in assessment of overdue fees.

MAY 1 9 2010

MAY 1 9 REC'D

AUG 0 6 2010

AUG 0 5 REC'D

DEC 1 5 2011

DEC

MAY 0 2 REC'D

FINES .50 | per day

Working After Welfare

How Women Balance Jobs and Family in the Wake of Welfare Reform

Kristin S. Seefeldt

2008

W.E. Upjohn Institute for Employment Research
Kalamazoo, Michigan

Library of Congress Cataloging-in-Publication Data

Seefeldt, Kristin S.
  Working after welfare : how women balance jobs and family in the wake of welfare reform / Kristin S. Seefeldt.
    p. cm.
  Includes bibliographical references and index.
  ISBN-13: 978-0-88099-344-9 (pbk. : alk. paper)
  ISBN-10: 0-88099-344-8 (pbk. : alk. paper)
  ISBN-13: 978-0-88099-345-6 (hardcover : alk. paper)
  ISBN-10: 0-88099-345-6 (hardcover : alk. paper)
  1. Welfare recipients—United States. 2. Working mothers—United States. 3. Public welfare—United States. I. Title.

HV91.S315 2008
306.3'6—dc22

                              2008049746

The facts presented in this study and the observations and viewpoints expressed are the sole responsibility of the author. They do not necessarily represent positions of the W.E. Upjohn Institute for Employment Research.

Cover design by Alcorn Publication Design.
Index prepared by Nairn Chadwick.
Printed in the United States of America.
Printed on recycled paper.

To Howard and Johnnie Mae Seeley,
who have cared for many over the years.

Contents

Figures

Tables

Acknowledgments

None of the work represented in this book could have been accomplished without the assistance of a great many organizations and individuals. First, the development of the Women's Employment Study (WES) and the collection and analysis of the data would not have been possible without the support of numerous funders. The Joyce Foundation, Charles Stewart Mott Foundation, the John D. and Catherine T. MacArthur Foundation, the Substance Abuse Policy Research Program of the Robert Wood Johnson Foundation, the National Institute of Child Health and Human Development, and the National Institute of Mental Health all provided support. The qualitative interviews could not have been conducted without the generous support of the Ford Foundation and the W.E. Upjohn Institute for Employment Research. In particular, I want to acknowledge my project officers at the Ford Foundation and Upjohn Institute, Helen Neuborne and Timothy Bartik. Kevin Hollenbeck, also at the Upjohn Institute, showed much-appreciated patience with me when my own work-family challenges mounted as I was revising the manuscript. Richard Wyrwa and the editorial staff at Upjohn made the text much more readable.

Sandra Danziger, the Principal Investigator of the WES, deserves special recognition for her leadership in shepherding the project over the years and providing unfailing support for my research. Without the efforts of the data collection team from the Survey Research Center at the Institute for Social Research (University of Michigan), we would not have the high-quality study that we do. Bruce Medbury, the survey manager for the first four waves of data collection, taught us all so much about how to do this type of work. Eva Leissou managed the final wave of data collection. Eva also was instrumental in launching the qualitative study, helping me with sample selection and allowing me access to the final wave of survey data as it was coming in from the field.

The qualitative interviews were a group effort. I started this project with my colleague and dear friend, Rukmalie Jayakody. As I began to move in my own direction with this work, she gave me the space and support to do so. Amber Arellano, Deogracia Cornelio, and Grace Okrah conducted many of the interviews, and the passion they brought to the task is still greatly appreciated. Joanna Parnes perfectly transcribed all of the interviews, compiled any and all information I needed from the survey, and helped me greatly with the management of the project. Over the course of the study, Rodney Andrews, Brian Cadena, Robin Phinney, and Alex Resch all worked with me or helped me resolve issues I faced with the survey data.

This book has benefited tremendously from the comments and suggestions of others. Elena Delbanco provided much-needed feedback and support when

I was struggling. My husband, Greg Levine, helped me see when I was being long-winded. David Morse and three anonymous reviewers also provided extremely useful comments on the first full draft. But foremost, I need to thank Sheldon Danziger, who read, edited, and reread various drafts, helped flesh out half-formed ideas, and left me alone to write when I needed that.

Finally, the individuals who were part of the WES need to be thanked, even if they never read this book or any of the other publications that have come out of the research. The women with whom we worked opened their homes to strangers from the University of Michigan and shared some of their most personal stories. We learned so much from them, and it is my hope that in some small way, their experiences will make a difference to the policy community.

1
Moving from Welfare to Work

In 2005 and 2006, the *New York Times* ran a number of articles about women's choices regarding motherhood, careers, and the balance between the two. "Many Women at Elite Colleges Set Career Path to Motherhood," claimed one article, citing a "trend" among female Ivy League students to say that they would rather be stay-at-home mothers than leaders in business, medicine, or other sectors.[1] A history professor quoted in the publication noted that these young women were "being realistic" about the difficulty of combining motherhood and work. Others mentioned in the article doubted the judgment of high-powered career women with children. One young woman commented, "I see a lot of women in their thirties who have full-time nannies, and I just question if their kids are getting the best."

"Stretched to the Limit, Women Stall March to Work" was the headline of another article, appearing in the *Times'* business section (Porter 2006). Women such as Cathie Watson-Short, 37, a former executive in the high-tech industry of California's Silicon Valley who decided to stay at home with her children, were profiled about their challenges balancing work and family obligations, with the latter often winning out. Watson-Short was quoted in the article as saying, "Most of us thought we would work and have kids, at least that was what we were brought up thinking we would do—no problem. But really we were kind of duped. None of us realized how hard it is."

Embedded within the "Stretched to Limit" article were three sentences acknowledging that a particular group of women, single mothers, posed an exception to the "trend" away from paid work in the formal economy toward staying at home with children. Welfare reform, along with other policy changes, the article noted, had helped fuel an increase in single mothers' labor force participation, from about 62 percent in 1995 to about 73 percent in 2000. The low work effort of single mothers receiving welfare was headline news and at the top of the nation's political agenda in the early to mid-1990s. Bill Clinton, in his first campaign for president, had pledged to "end welfare as we know it," and by

1996, the nation's cash welfare system had been overhauled from one that issued checks to poor single mothers to one that made receipt of benefits contingent upon looking for and getting a job (Weaver 2000).

However, 10 years after the passage of welfare reform, the media and policymakers are paying less attention to the situation of former welfare recipients who entered the labor force compared to women like those highlighted by the *Times*. Single mothers who earn low wages cannot afford nannies, and child care is expensive. Yet, reducing their work effort is not a viable option after the 1996 welfare reform.

In this volume, I hope to share some insights about the lives of single mothers who left welfare for work. They experience struggles similar to those faced by women profiled by the *Times*, yet they have far fewer resources. Most of the women whose situations I have studied have not attended college, let alone Ivy League institutions, and few have spouses or other partners to help with child rearing. These individuals include Mishon, a hotel housekeeper in her early thirties with two teenagers.[2] In 2004, Mishon earned just over the minimum wage. Mishon's hours at work had recently been reduced, but she believed it was better for her to stay with her current employer, since her schedule was otherwise stable, allowing her time to help her children with their homework. At the other end of the spectrum in terms of pay is Caroline, who by 2004 was earning the equivalent of $19 an hour as a registered nurse. Yet, Caroline also did not want to switch jobs, in her case to a supervisory position, fearing that she would lose control over her schedule and have to work when others called in sick or the like. Although Caroline admitted that she probably had more flexibility to work different shifts (third shift, for example), now that her three children were older, she too contended that her children "came first" in all of her decisions.

Mishon and Caroline were part of the Women's Employment Study (WES), originally designed by researchers at the University of Michigan to follow about 750 welfare recipients as they attempted to make the transition from welfare to work. Participants in the WES were surveyed five times (1997, 1998, 1999, 2001, and 2003). In-depth interviews were conducted in 2004 with some members of the study, including Mishon and Caroline, who had found jobs and had more or less remained steadily employed. While these women are typically considered as the "successes" of welfare reform, many faced challenges in moving up the economic ladder. Some found it difficult to obtain jobs that paid higher wages or to find opportunities to increase their skills and thus their employment possibilities. A large body of research, some of it presented in the next two chapters, focused on the employment obstacles of welfare recipients, including low education levels, lack of work experience, and mental and physical health problems (Corcoran, Danziger, and Tolman 2004; Danziger et al. 2000; Olson and Pavetti 1996; Zedlewski 2003). However, aside from education, issues such as these were rarely discussed by the women we interviewed.

Rather, women talked about their responsibilities on the job and their perceptions of the work environment; some found meaning and dignity in their employment, while others described workplaces rife with favoritism, discrimination, and sometimes harassment. Many women also struggled to balance work and family demands, and spoke of these tensions using language similar to that of middle- and upper-income career women such as Cathie Watson-Short, the individual profiled by the *New York Times*. Yet, the policies that are in place to address work-family balance issues tend to benefit those who work in well-paid jobs. For example, the Family and Medical Leave Act (FMLA) of 1997 requires employers to provide up to 12 weeks of leave to certain classes of employees so that they can perform specific caretaking responsibilities (such as for a newborn or an ill family member). However, that time is unpaid, and workers in low-wage jobs, particularly single mothers who are sole earners for their families, usually cannot afford lengthy absences without pay. Further, to qualify for FMLA's benefits, employees must have been working in the job for at least 12 months. Higher-than-average turnover characterizes the low-wage labor market, so many mothers may not work in one job long enough to be eligible for unpaid leave.

To the extent that policy addresses the family lives of low-wage workers and welfare recipients in particular, it is often through proposals to increase the availability and quality of child care. However, many women in the WES took very seriously their roles as mothers and spoke of a strong desire to participate in their children's lives and activities, not just have them spend time in formal day care. Like the high-income mothers profiled in another *New York Times* article, "The Time Trap" (Hulbert 2006), women in the WES were shuttling children to and from sports practices and other extracurricular activities. However, unlike higher-income mothers, who might "commiserate" about the "perfect madness of child rearing," the women in our study were constrained by an inflexible low-wage labor market. Their trade-off was not whether to work or to stay home and raise children, but one of finding the right balance between caregiving responsibilities and their families' financial needs. Once that equilibrium was struck, many women chose to remain in a job, even if that meant stagnant or slow wage growth. In fact, numerous respondents were hesitant to take promotions or to return to school, activities that could help them advance in the job market, for fear of disrupting their children's schedules and/or because of an unwillingness to spend less time with their families.

The stories reported here paint a portrait of the lives of women who, although employed primarily in the low-wage labor market, are dealing with issues that are common to other working mothers. The policy discourse around making the workplace more "friendly" to parents needs to move beyond white-collar jobs, often held by married mothers, to the labor market as a whole, acknowledging the special challenges faced by low-income single parents while also granting them the same respect for their role as that given to other parents.

However, policies directed toward single mothers are very often linked to the welfare system and not to the labor market. Most notable was the 1996 welfare reform, which many have credited with moving women like Mishon and Caroline into jobs. The desire to learn more about the trajectories of welfare recipients after the law's passage was the impetus for launching the WES. The remainder of this chapter presents additional information on the welfare system as it operated in the mid-to-late 1990s, the time period when the WES began data collection, in order to provide a sense of the policy environment faced by women in this study.

A BRIEF OVERVIEW OF THE WELFARE SYSTEM

Fueled by rising cash assistance caseloads, state experimentation with program design, and presidential candidate Clinton's 1992 pledge to "end welfare as we know it," the nation's cash welfare program, Aid to Families with Dependent Children (AFDC), was radically reformed. Passage of the Personal Responsibility and Work Opportunity Reconciliation Act (PRWORA) in 1996 marked a significant redesign of a welfare system that had started as a small New Deal program to serve widows and their children. However, AFDC evolved into providing ongoing income support to more than five million families by the mid-1990s, most of which were headed by never-married mothers. Today, receipt of cash welfare is no longer an open-ended entitlement, as symbolized by the name of the program that replaced AFDC—Temporary Assistance to Needy Families (TANF)—and the federal prohibition against receipt of TANF for more than 60 months in a recipient's life. Although this was perhaps one of the most controversial features of the law, in practice, relatively few recipients have been affected by time limits (Bloom, Ferrell, and Fink 2002).[3]

Work requirements and penalties for failing to comply with these and other program rules are also hallmarks of the "reformed" welfare system. States and recipients must meet "work participation" guidelines. From a state's perspective, a certain proportion of the caseload, regardless of the length of time a recipient has received aid, must be working or participating in a work-related activity (e.g., looking for a job, receiving short-term training in how to find a job, and, on a limited basis, participating in a short-term training program that prepares the recipient for a specific job). Beginning in 1997, 25 percent of families had to be in a work activity, and the proportion increased to 50 percent in 2002. Recipients had to participate in work activities no later than 24 months after first coming onto the rolls. Hours required for single parents to meet the work requirement increased from 20 per week in 1997 to 30 per week in 2000.[4]

As a way to enforce participation in work activities, states must sanction or penalize recipients by reducing their benefit amount for noncompliance with employment or other program requirements. Although sanctioning predates the 1996 welfare reform, PRWORA mandates that states implement sanction policies and also allows states to eliminate benefits altogether. Each state (and sometimes locality) determines noncompliance differently. In general, though, not attending required activities (such as employment programs), not making a good faith effort in finding a job, or quitting or being fired may result in a sanction.

More than a decade after PRWORA was passed, welfare use is quite low, and with few exceptions, the program receives relatively little political or media attention. As Figure 1.1 shows, welfare caseloads, which peaked in early 1994, as of 2003 were at the lowest levels in more than 30 years, with approximately two million families receiving assistance. Employment levels for less-educated single mothers (not shown in the figure) also reached record highs, despite a recession in the early 2000s. Yet, as seen in the figure, the number of female-headed households living in poverty declined at a slower rate than welfare caseloads in the 1990s, and even rose from 2000 to 2003, suggesting that many former welfare recipients remain in low-wage jobs and/or work intermittently throughout the year.

Although numerous analyses on the well-being of families who left welfare were conducted postreform, information on their longer-run outcomes is limited, particularly on the challenges these mothers face balancing work and family while navigating the low-wage labor mar-

Figure 1.1 Welfare Cases and Female-Headed Households in Poverty, 1959–2003 (in millions)

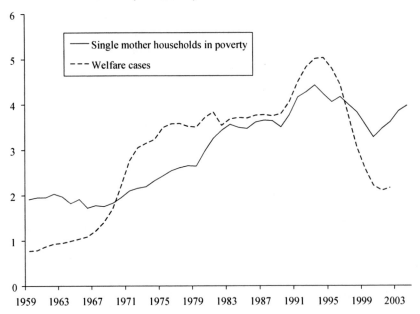

SOURCE: Author's tabulations of U.S. census data and data from the U.S. Department of Health and Human Services.

ket. Initial studies concluded that, although a majority of former welfare recipients were working at any given point in time, most were employed in low-wage jobs. However, a key tenet of many state welfare-to-work programs was that these low-paying, low-skilled jobs were the necessary stepping-off point for welfare recipients. For example, in Michigan, the state's work program, Work First, had as its mantra, "A job, a better job, a career." Other policymakers used the metaphor of a ladder to describe the perceived progression of welfare recipients in the labor market. This approach, whereby a better job is obtained through more work experience, represented a shift from the conventional wisdom about the need for recipients to participate in education and training activities in order to advance and achieve self-sufficiency.

THE ROLE OF EDUCATION IN THE WELFARE SYSTEM

An earlier version of welfare reform, the Family Support Act (FSA) of 1988, encouraged welfare recipients to participate in activities such as basic education, high school completion, vocational skills training, and, in some states, postsecondary education. However, by the mid-1990s, education and training programs were starting to come under fire.

First, at any point in time, relatively few welfare recipients were engaged in any type of job preparation activity, including education. The centerpiece of the FSA was the Job Opportunity and Basic Skills (JOBS) program, which was designed to move welfare recipients off welfare and into gainful employment. It emphasized participation in basic or in postsecondary education, or in other schooling and training, with the notion being that this accumulation of learning, or "human capital," would allow welfare recipients to compete for and secure good jobs. However, the rules allowed states to exempt large proportions of the welfare caseload, including mothers of children under age six, the disabled, and those living in remote locations, from participating in the JOBS program. A recession in the early 1990s also constrained states' abilities to fully fund the program. In fiscal year 1994, less than half of all AFDC recipients were classified as mandatory JOBS participants, and only about 21 percent of those were participating in an activity (U.S. House of Representatives 1996).

At the same time, evaluation results of various welfare-to-work program approaches were interpreted as documenting not only the weakness of education and training but also the strength of a work first approach as a way of moving recipients off assistance. In particular, the Riverside, California, Greater Avenues for Independence (GAIN) program, which had a strong emphasis on finding work (including linking staff performance evaluations to the number of clients placed in employment), was frequently cited by policymakers as an exemplar of this approach. Riverside was one of several California counties participating in an appraisal of various welfare-to-work programs. Compared to the other counties, Riverside achieved greater success, measured in terms of earnings of welfare recipients and savings to the welfare offices.[5]

Many states pursued the Riverside model, moving away from the education and training philosophy initially pursued under JOBS and implementing Work First programs. Some states also sought waivers to experiment with their welfare systems. Under Section 1115 of the Social Security Act, states could request federal approval to deviate from federal regulations for AFDC in order to test out new rules and policies, including work first approaches. During the debates leading up to welfare reform, quick attachment to the labor market came to be viewed as one of the solutions to the "problem" of welfare.

In the end, PRWORA's work requirements were perceived by most state policymakers to leave little room for placing recipients in education and training programs. In addition to the employment requirements that have been described, the law specifies that no more than 30 percent of TANF recipients can participate in vocational training programs and have that activity counted toward the federal work requirement. Further, federal dollars may only be used for short-term training programs of a year or less. Finally, participation in postsecondary education is not an "allowable" activity, meaning that recipients in college may not be counted toward the work requirement, and federal dollars may not be used to support college attendance.

EMPLOYMENT ASSISTANCE UNDER WELFARE REFORM

While support for education and training efforts was greatly curtailed in the wake of PRWORA, nearly all states sought to provide employment assistance to welfare recipients in the form of Work First programs. Although the details of each state's program vary (and may differ greatly within each state), Work First programs under PRWORA aim to assist clients in finding employment quickly, as opposed to placing them initially in education and training activities.

In Michigan, an applicant for TANF, called the Family Independence Program (FIP), would come to her local welfare office, the Family Independence Agency (FIA), fill out application forms, meet with or schedule an appointment with a caseworker for an application interview, and then be referred to a "joint orientation."[6] The JO, as referred to by many workers, introduced the "new" welfare system in Michigan. Representatives from the FIA and from the Work First program provided an overview of the many services a woman could receive by participating in Work First, such as assistance with transportation (at one time this aid included car repairs and help with purchasing a vehicle), referrals to various community agencies, and, most important, help in finding a job. In return for this assistance, recipients had to accept "rights and responsibilities," including agreeing to comply with various program rules and to take suitable employment.

Attendance at the orientation was part of the welfare application process. That is, new applicants (among others) would not have their TANF case processed for eligibility unless they attended JO. PowerPoint presentations were developed by the state to facilitate these sessions, and some localities brought in representatives from local social service agencies, whose offerings (child care, transportation, domestic violence and other counseling) recipients might need. After orientation, applicants were expected to start the Work First program within the next week or two, in some cases before they had been deemed eligible for welfare benefits.

The Work First program in Michigan is operated by the state labor department, first called the Michigan Jobs Commission (MJC), later the Department of Workforce Development (DWD), and currently the Department of Labor and Economic Growth (DLEG). The state agency transfers TANF funds, as well as decision-making authority, to local workforce development boards and their administrative entities, the Michigan Works! Agencies (MWAs). The boards and the MWAs then contract out for actual service provision. Work First is primarily run by not-for-profit entities, including Goodwill and local community organizations. However, a number of for-profit companies, including some operating in multiple states, also hold Work First contracts.

During the early years of program operations, typical Work First activities included workshops on a variety of "job readiness" skills.[7] Classes were designed to teach skills deemed necessary to search for employment but not necessarily those needed on a job. Most programs included brief sessions on interviewing techniques, resume and cover letter preparation, and how to "dress for success." After that, clients typically had three weeks to search for work (Seefeldt, Danziger, and Danziger 2003). Depending upon where they lived, participants received varying degrees of assistance in this task. Some programs required recipients to look for positions on their own, reflecting beliefs that 1) people will stay longer in jobs they find for themselves, and 2) learning how to find work is just as important as working. Other programs offered "hands-on" assistance, such as calling employers on clients' behalf or bringing employers to the program or to the welfare office to conduct interviews on site.

How many welfare recipients actually received services from Work First is unclear. During fiscal year 1998 (October 1997–September 1998), the second year of the program post–welfare reform, about 36 percent of referrals to Work First never attended the program. Statewide, about 46 percent of participants secured employment (Michigan Jobs Commission 1998). However, while attendance at orientation was mandatory for all applicants for assistance, not all were necessarily expected to participate in the program's job search and related activities. For example, recipients with newborns were excused from participation, as were women who received disability benefits from the Supplemental Security Income (SSI) program or who cared for children receiving SSI. Some welfare recipients were already employed; they fulfilled program requirements by attending orientation and then continuing to work at their jobs.

On the other hand, some employed women were instructed to attend the actual program, and their jobs were counted toward Work First placement rates. Another group of welfare recipients, though, simply never showed up at the sessions after orientation. Some portion of this group may have decided to find work on their own. An often-heard complaint from participants, both in Michigan and in other states, was that these programs did not teach them anything they did not already know. Certain recipients, then, may have decided the program was a waste of time and applied for work on their own. Some Work First staff worried that the jobs the recipients found themselves might not pay as well or be as good a match as the positions that the Work First agency could help them find. Other Work First staff were satisfied to count those participants—even if they never attended the program—as "employed" in their statistics.

Along with Work First programs, a number of other supports are theoretically available to individuals to assist them as they leave welfare for employment. First, federal funding for child care was consolidated and the levels increased dramatically after welfare reform (Fuller et al. 2002). These monies were not just to be used for welfare recipients but also for individuals in low-income families needing child care assistance in order to work. In the early 2000s, the care of an estimated two million children was at least partially subsidized by these funds (Adams and Rohacek 2002). Securing safe, reliable, and quality child care is a challenge for many working parents, but low-wage workers may face particular issues, such as finding quality care at a price they can afford (state or federal subsidies rarely cover the full cost), or, if they work nonstandard hours, finding child care that is available when they need it.

The Earned Income Tax Credit, or EITC, is not a welfare policy, but it provides a strong employment incentive to low-wage workers, including welfare recipients. Working families with children who earn approximately $35,000 a year or less can qualify for the EITC. The size of the EITC varies by earnings. For a family with two or more children, the EITC rises as earnings increase up to about $12,000, flattens, and then begins to phase out around $16,000. The maximum EITC benefit (in 2005) for a family with two children was about $4,400; for a family with just one child, it was about $2,600. Workers whose income tax liability is less than the amount of the credit for which they qualify receive the remaining amount of the credit as a refund (see Greenstein [2005] for an overview of the EITC and its antipoverty effectiveness).

AFTER WORK FIRST: CAREER ADVANCEMENT

After welfare reform, record numbers of single mothers, including many recipients, found jobs. According to the U.S. Department of Labor (2008a), the proportion of single mothers who were employed was nearly 70 percent in 2004, surpassing the rate of married mothers, just under two-thirds of whom were employed. However, many policymakers and advocates have noted that simply moving women from welfare into work would not make their families self-sufficient. Numerous states undertook "welfare leavers" studies. Although their methodologies varied and the time frames were not consistent, most reports found that at any point, only about 60 percent of former recipients were still working. Returns to welfare were not uncommon, suggesting that at least some women who had left such support with a job no longer had one. Among those employed, wages remained low—about $7 to $8 an hour.[8]

In order to help former recipients maintain employment and advance, states began offering services ranging from transportation assistance and counseling to handle workplace disputes—support that might help workers keep existing jobs—to opportunities to participate in vocational training activities in order to secure better jobs.[9] These "postemployment services" were tested and evaluated in a national demonstration project prior to welfare reform. Mathematica Policy Research, a social welfare policy evaluation firm, examined four programs that provided a variety of services, including individualized counseling to employed welfare recipients. Participation in the program, however, seemed to make little difference in rates of employment and level of earnings (Rangarajan and Novak 1999). Other programs providing postemployment or retention services have had difficulties recruiting participants, with some evidence indicating that clients were not interested in the offerings (Anderson and Martinson 2003; Hill, Kirby, and Fraker 2001).

Michigan started offering postemployment services, particularly opportunities to receive further skills training, in 1999. The state developed the "10-10-10" program, named for the number of hours welfare recipients could combine employment (10 hours), training (10 hours), and study time (10 hours) to fulfill the work requirement. Similar to the experiences of other states, enrollment was very low. According to state administrative data for fiscal year 2002 (October 2001–September 2002), just under 4 percent of all Work First participants were in an education or training activity (Michigan Department of Labor and Economic Growth 2003). Program operators cited difficulties in finding employers who would schedule recipients for only 10 hours of work per week and the lack of time on the part of clients who found it difficult to juggle work, school, and family responsibilities (Seefeldt et al. 2001).

Work First providers, who operated under yearly or biannual contracts, may have also lacked incentives to help recipients find jobs that accommodated participation in training programs. Although the 10-10-10 program and allowances for postemployment services were implemented at the state level, providers were evaluated locally by the numbers of recipients who became employed, not by the number in training programs.

What, then, happened to women who left welfare for work? Did they find jobs on their own? Did they keep these jobs? Did they experience the slogan of Work First—"A job, a better job, a career"? These questions are addressed in the following chapters. Chapter 2 describes the WES sample, using information from the surveys that were administered over a six-year period. This chapter will give the reader a sense of the challenges faced by women who participated in the study, including mental health problems, domestic violence, and low levels of education. Chapter 3 uses the WES survey data to examine the employment trajectories experienced by women who went to work shortly after welfare reform. I use the rich survey data to examine which of the various personal and family issues are associated with certain pathways, such as moving from a job with a very low wage to one paying a higher wage or remaining employed in very low-paying positions. In the remaining chapters, I draw upon data from in-depth interviews that were conducted with a subsample of WES respondents after completion of the surveys. Chapter 4 describes in more detail how women embarked on their employment pathways, the choices they made, and various obstacles and opportunities encountered along the way. Chapter 5 expands upon these findings, detailing the attributes of jobs that women in the study considered to be most beneficial and detrimental to their well-being and their assessments of their current jobs on these dimensions. Chapter 6 examines women's pathways to employment advancement, noting the real and perceived hindrances to upward mobility and the trade-offs women made to balance work and family. In the final chapter, I discuss some policy options that could increase the financial well-being of single mothers and support the role that parenthood plays in their lives.

Notes

1. This article, written by Louise Story, appeared on the front page of the *New York Times* on September 20, 2005. Economist Claudia Goldin (2006) disputes the "opting out" trend, arguing that data do not support these stories.
2. Names of women in the study have been changed to protect their confidentiality.
3. States may specify certain exemption and extension categories to the time limit, for example, for women experiencing domestic abuse, but the number of families with such exemptions must not exceed 20 percent of the state's average monthly caseload. States can continue to support families past 60 months using their own funds.
4. PRWORA needed to be reauthorized in 2002, but Congress did not do so until 2005. Welfare reauthorization maintained the 50 percent participation rate for states. However, the types of activities that now count toward the work requirement have been narrowed.
5. However, many recipients in Riverside did participate in training and other educational-type programs. Moreover, evaluators of GAIN speculated that it was not any one factor that accounted for the county's success, but a combination of welfare office practices and other conditions that might not be replicable in other areas (Seefeldt 2002).
6. The Family Independence Agency (FIA) was changed to the Department of Human Services (DHS) in 2005, a name closely resembling its previous incarnation, the Department of Social Services, which was changed to FIA in 1997.
7. In 2005, the state of Michigan began to redesign its employment program for welfare recipients. Although Work First is still operating in parts of the state as of early 2008, a new program is being phased in: Jobs, Education, and Training (JET).
8. For an overview of findings from state leaver studies, see Acs and Loprest (2004).
9. A small number of states, including California and Maine, allowed some recipients to attend community colleges as a way to meet the TANF work requirements (U.S. House of Representatives 1996).

2

Six Years Later, How Are Former Welfare Recipients Faring in the Labor Market?

As debates over how to reform welfare were drawing to a close, it became clear to many observers that social policy affecting poor families was about to change dramatically. Questions were raised as to whether most welfare recipients, many of whom lacked a high school diploma or any significant work experience, would be able to obtain jobs that could support their families. Some expected the new law to drive many households into poverty. For example, analyses conducted by the Urban Institute, a Washington-based research organization, estimated that an additional one million children would become poor as a result of welfare reform (Weaver 2000).

In response to these concerns, a number of teams launched major research projects designed to track the well-being of recipients postreform. One of these, the WES, a collaborative effort among a multidisciplinary group of University of Michigan researchers, collected data from a sample of Michigan women who received cash welfare in early 1997, just after welfare reform was implemented in that state.[1] Since WES data serve as the basis of the findings presented in this book, in this chapter I provide background information on the study and use the survey data to begin to answer the question, "Six years later, how are former recipients faring?"

OVERVIEW OF THE WOMEN'S EMPLOYMENT STUDY

The WES is a panel survey that began in 1997 and followed a random sample of welfare recipients from one urban Michigan county, collecting five waves of survey data. The initial sample consisted of 875 women receiving TANF as single-parent cases.[2] All women were between the ages of 18 and 54 when the study began, received TANF in February 1997, and were African American or white U.S. citizens.[3] Surveys lasted about one hour in duration at the first wave in 1997, about 85 minutes at the later waves, and were conducted in person, primarily in the women's homes.

Response rates at each wave were uniformly high, ranging from 86 percent at wave 1 (1997) to 93 percent at the fifth wave in 2003. For all survey data shown in this book, I report on the 536 women who remained in the survey at all five waves. They represent 71 percent of the original 753 who took part in the wave 1 survey. Although more than one-third of the sample was lost due to attrition (mostly due to an inability to locate respondents, who moved frequently, rather than refusals to participate further), analyses indicate that any differences between women who stayed in the sample through 2003 and women who left earlier are not substantively significant (Cadena and Pape 2006).

Table 2.1 shows the basic demographic characteristics of individuals in the sample when they were first interviewed in 1997 and again at the last survey in 2003.[4] On average, women were about 30 years old when first interviewed, and, as would be expected, were about 36 years old in 2003. About 55 percent were African American, and the other participants were white. On average, they had about two children living at home with them. Although some women gave birth during the study period, other women had children leave home or turn 18, with the net effect of very little change in the number of resident children between 1997 and 2003.

At every survey wave (1997, 1998, 1999, 2001, 2003), the WES gathered information on labor market experiences, income, mental health problems (such as depression, posttraumatic stress disorder, al-

Table 2.1 WES Sample Characteristics (*n* = 536)

	1997 (Wave 1)	2003 (Wave 5)
Average age	30.3	36.3
African American (%)	54.7	54.7
White (%)	45.3	45.3
Total number of children at home	2.1	2.0
Married (%)	11.0	20.2

SOURCE: Author's tabulations from WES data.

cohol dependence, and drug dependence based on criteria established by the American Psychiatric Association's *Diagnostic and Statistical Manual of Mental Disorders [DSM-IV]*), maternal and child health problems, experiences of domestic violence, and household and family composition. A primary goal of the study was to examine the movement from welfare to work and the role that potential employment barriers play in that transition. To date, the study has found that significant proportions of women had hindrances to employment such as lack of transportation, limited education, low literacy, depression, and child care problems. Additionally, having multiple impediments significantly reduced the likelihood of employment, and having persistent obstacles increased the likelihood of remaining on or returning to welfare (Danziger et al. 2000; Seefeldt and Orzol 2005). On the other hand, the majority of WES respondents worked in any given month, with average employment rates ranging from 60 to 70 percent. For those who worked, earnings increased over time, although many did not earn their way out of poverty. Unstable employment patterns were characteristic of just under half of all workers (Danziger et al. 2002; Johnson and Corcoran 2003).

WELFARE USE AND EMPLOYMENT RATES

Figure 2.1 displays the trends in welfare and food stamp use and employment rates among WES respondents.[5] As noted earlier, when the study began in February 1997, all (100 percent) sample members were receiving cash assistance through Michigan's TANF program, the Family Independence Program (FIP). At that time, though, just over two-fifths, 43.5 percent, were combining welfare with work. Michigan allows TANF recipients to keep the first $200 per month and 20 percent of the remaining amount of earnings before dollar-for-dollar deductions are made from the welfare grant.

Receipt of welfare among respondents, as measured by state administrative data, plummeted sharply over the next several years, mirroring trends at the national level. The proportion of the sample receiving TANF during the period 2001–2004 hovered around 20 percent. Many of those who continued to receive welfare and remained on the rolls for

Figure 2.1 Percent of WES Sample Working, Receiving Welfare (FIP) and Food Assistance, by Month, February 1997–August 2004 (n = 503)

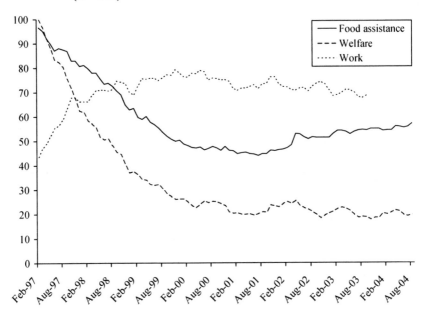

NOTE: Wave 5 non-SSI recipients only.
SOURCE: Author's tabulations from WES data.

most of the months during the study period tended to have persistent physical health problems, children with ongoing health problems, and/ or larger families (Seefeldt and Orzol 2005).

However, most of the sample left welfare by 2003 and did not return. Many of these women worked in at least some months during a year. Employment rates among the sample climbed steadily throughout 1997 and 1998 and reached a peak in November 1999, when nearly 80 percent of the women were employed. After that date, smaller proportions of women were employed in each month. In August 2003, the last month for which we have employment data for all respondents, just over two-thirds, 68.6 percent, were employed.[6]

As employment rates fell, use of the Food Stamp program started to rise. Between 1997 and 2001, participation in the program declined, but not as quickly as participation in cash welfare. The Food Stamp program has long been viewed as a support for working poor families, and eligibility limits for receipt of this benefit are higher than those for cash welfare. For example, in 2000, a single mother in Michigan with two children who worked full time for the full year at $7 an hour would not receive any assistance through TANF, but her family would be eligible for $91 a month in food stamps.[7] Although analyses of WES data to date have not examined the correlates of food stamp use, particularly returns to food stamps, the data presented in Figure 2.1 indicate at least some association between the economic downturn in early 2001 and increased use of food stamps.

In sum, WES respondents, like welfare recipients throughout the nation, left the cash assistance rolls in great numbers after the 1996 welfare reform. Many of these women found employment or increased their work effort. Although the slowdown of the economy in 2001 went along with decreased employment rates, the majority of respondents remained off welfare and in the labor force. For many of us working on the WES, this was surprising given the high rates of employment challenges faced by welfare recipients.

EMPLOYMENT CHALLENGES

Although programs like Work First, described in Chapter 1, were designed to link welfare recipients to available jobs, many observers worried that the types of opportunities available to recipients would be low paying and would leave women unable to support their families. Further, surveys of employers, most notably those undertaken by economist Harry Holzer, showed that, even for entry-level job openings, workers were desired to have high school diplomas and the ability to perform simple reading and computational tasks (Holzer 1996). Yet, many welfare recipients lacked these credentials. Employers may also look for a strong prior attachment to the labor market as a signal of the ability to perform a variety of job-related tasks or as a proxy for the ability to show up to work reliably. Another concern was that welfare recipients who had minimal work histories were perhaps not accustomed to the "culture" of work (Berg, Olsen, and Conrad 1991).

Finally, discrimination may affect welfare mothers' success in the labor market. First, studies conducted in the early 1990s found that some employers held negative views of African Americans and residents of inner cities (Moss and Tilly 2001; Neckerman and Kirschenman 1991) and of African American single mothers more generally (Kennelly 1999). These attitudes, if widespread, might mean that welfare recipients have a harder time convincing employers to hire them. Also, as Kalil et al. (1998) note, experiencing such discrimination may make welfare recipients "less willing to search widely for jobs" (p. 8).

When first interviewed, many WES respondents had a number of human capital "deficits." As shown in Table 2.2, about 30 percent of respondents reported that they had neither completed high school nor had obtained a GED (general educational development certificate). In 2001, we administered the Washington State Screener for Learning Disabilities, which has been widely used as an indicator of a learning disability. About 13 percent of respondents scored as having a learning disability.[8]

To measure work skills, respondents were asked whether or not they had performed any of nine tasks on their previous jobs on a daily, weekly, or monthly basis. These skills include working on a computer, writing letters or memos, watching gauges or dials, speaking with customers face-to-face, speaking with customers on the phone, reading instructions, filling out forms, doing arithmetic, and working with machines. Performance of fewer than four of these tasks led to classification of having a skills barrier for about 20 percent of the sample. Low

Table 2.2 Human Capital Deficits for the WES Sample as Measured in 1997 (*n* = 536)

Human capital characteristics	%
Less than high school education/no GED	29.9
Learning disability	13.3
Low work experience	13.9
Work skills barrier	21.1
Work norms barrier	8.9
Prior discrimination	14.7
Any human capital deficit	61.9

SOURCE: Author's tabulations from WES data.

work experience was defined as working in less than 20 percent of one's adult years: 14 percent of the sample had this human capital deficit.

Respondents were also asked to evaluate the appropriateness of nine different work-related scenarios: missing work without calling in, not correcting a problem pointed out by a supervisor, coming to work late, making personal calls on the job, arguing with customers, leaving work early without approval, taking a longer-than-scheduled break, refusing to do tasks outside one's job description, and not getting along with a supervisor. Women who reported that engaging in at least five of these behaviors "would not be a serious problem" were coded as not knowing workplace norms. Anecdotally, many staff in Work First programs complained that welfare recipients did not know about appropriate workplace behavior. However, even though a research study conducted in a very low-income inner city housing project indicated that this was a significant problem among those sampled (Berg, Olsen, and Conrad 1991), only about 9 percent of our sample lacked understanding of the seriousness of such acts.

About 15 percent of women in our study reported that they had experienced some form of discrimination on a prior or current job. Experiences of discrimination were measured by 16 questions, adapted from a Los Angeles neighborhood survey (Bobo and Suh 2000), tapping into various dimensions including whether women thought they had ever been refused a job, fired, or not been promoted due to their gender, race, or welfare status; whether their supervisor made racial slurs or said insulting remarks about women or welfare recipients; whether they believed they had been discriminated against on the job more generally due to their race, gender, or welfare status; and whether they had been the victim of sexual harassment at work.

Many evaluations of welfare-to-work programs have noted that welfare recipients, in addition to having relatively low human capital, face logistical challenges in moving to employment, with child care and transportation the two most commonly cited. By definition, welfare recipients must be the caregivers of children, and, particularly for mothers with very young children, going to work entails arranging child care. Depending upon where one lives, securing low-cost, reliable, and safe care may be extremely difficult. Further, finding help for children with health problems or other special needs may pose particular challenges due to the increased expense and the limited number of spaces for such attention. Additionally, as Olson and Pavetti (1996) note, mothers of children with special needs may be reluctant to leave them in a new environment.

Families with older children might also face care-related challenges. In interviews with welfare mothers living in several large cities, Edin and Lein (1997) find that many were concerned about their school-age and teenage children's safety while they were away at work. Some women lived in neighborhoods rife with gangs, while others were concerned that, left unattended, children might get into trouble, engage in sexual activity, and, if female, become pregnant. The WES did not ask directly about child care problems until later survey waves. As noted previously, the average woman in the study had two children; in 1997, just under two-thirds of the sample had preschool-age children, and more than two-fifths had children aged two or younger (Table 2.3). We would expect that women with children in these age groups would need to find day care if they were to go to work. Further, approximately 23 percent of the sample reported that at least one of their children had a physical health, learning, or emotional problem.

Getting to and from work may also present difficulties for low-income individuals who may not have the money to purchase or maintain a car. For welfare recipients living in larger cities and with access to public transportation, the lack of a car may not be as severe an impediment. However, a growing literature in the late 1990s documented a "spatial mismatch" between entry-level jobs, which were increasingly located in the suburbs, and a low-skilled labor pool, which was more concentrated in the inner cities (Stoll 2006). In Michigan, few areas support strong public transportation systems, so we classify respondents as having a transportation barrier if they lacked regular access to a car and/or they did not have a valid driver's license. In 1997, 43 percent of the sample lacked one or both.

While the prevalence of low education levels, spotty employment histories, and child care and transportation problems among recipients had been recognized well before the passage of welfare reform, a number of studies in the late 1990s, including the WES, showed that individuals faced other challenges (listed in Table 2.3) in moving from welfare to work. Specifically, compared to national samples of women, welfare recipients were more likely to suffer from depression and other

Table 2.3 Employment Challenges for the WES Sample as Measured in 1997 (_n_ = 536)

Challenge	%
Any preschool-aged children	64.6
Any children aged two or younger	41.8
Child with health problem	22.9
Transportation barrier	42.9
Any mental health problem	36.9
Depression	27.5
PTSD	15.5
Generalized anxiety disorder	7.5
Alcohol dependence	3.0
Drug dependence	4.3
Domestic violence	16.0
Drug use	22.0
Physical health problem	19.4

SOURCE: Author's tabulations from WES data.

mental health disorders and to have recently experienced domestic violence (Danziger et al. 2000). Women with mental health problems may lack the energy to search for employment, or the illness may interfere with being able to function while at work. The severe negative effects of domestic violence on women are numerous, but one recognized symptom is interference on the part of the abuser with women's efforts to go to work (Raphael 2000).

In 1997, 36.9 percent of WES respondents met the diagnostic screening criteria for at least one of five mental health problems (depression, generalized anxiety disorder, posttraumatic stress disorder, alcohol dependence, drug dependence). The prevalence of these disorders was assessed through the Composite International Diagnostic Interview used in the National Comorbidity Study, which uses questions designed to measure symptoms and conditions specified by the _DSM-IV_. Major depression was the most common disorder, with 27.5 percent of the sample meeting screening criteria, followed by posttraumatic stress disorder (15.5 percent), and generalized anxiety disorder (7.5 percent). Alcohol and drug dependence affected relatively small proportions of the sample, 3.0 and 4.3 percent, respectively.

In other studies, estimates of the proportion of welfare recipients with serious and/or functionally limiting physical health problems ranged from less than 10 percent to more than 30 percent (Olson and Pavetti 1996). Within the WES, just under one-fifth of women assessed their health as being fair or poor *and* scored in the lowest quartile for a variety of physical functioning tasks.[9]

The role of substance abuse problems in the life of welfare mothers is unclear. Depending upon the definition used, as few as 2 to 3 percent of recipients or as many as 37 percent may have some sort of substance-related problem (Pollack et al. 2002). While relatively few women met the psychiatric definition of alcohol or drug dependence, which considers both extent of use of the substances and reliance upon them for functioning, more respondents reported using drugs than meeting the criteria for drug dependence. Respondents were asked whether they had, in the previous 12 months, used an illegal substance (such as marijuana or cocaine) or used a prescription or over-the-counter medication on their own (e.g., without a prescription or without following directions regarding proper dosage). Just over one-fifth of the sample reported such use.

EMPLOYMENT AND EARNINGS

Given the extent of human capital and other employment challenges, the wages of those working at the wave 1 (1997) survey were relatively low—median hourly wage rates were $6.66 (in 2003 inflation-adjusted dollars). As shown in Figure 2.2, wage rates increased by 25 percent over the six-year study period, reaching a median of $8.35 an hour in 2003 (wage progression among the WES sample will be discussed in more detail in the next chapter). Many women held service jobs, such as cashiers in retail stores or fast-food outlets, janitors, or health care aides. By 2003, about half of all jobs were in services, which is not surprising given the growth in that sector in the economy as a whole. Although service jobs are typically characterized as low paying and dead-end, there are some reasons to believe that overall employment quality increased over time for women in the WES.

Figure 2.2 Median Hourly Wage among WES Workers (in 2003 $)

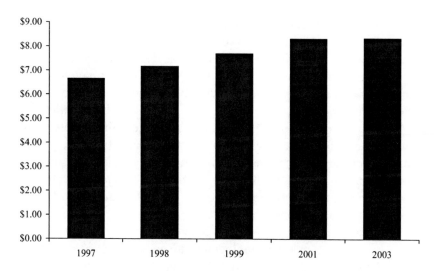

NOTE: The years shown represent the five survey periods.
SOURCE: Author's tabulations from WES data.

On a number of dimensions, we saw improvement in the types of jobs women held. First, in 2003, 16.6 percent of workers were in positions covered by a union or a collective bargaining agreement, up from 11 percent in 1997. Although comparable national data are not available on the proportion of former welfare recipients in union jobs, it is likely that given Michigan's history as a union stronghold, the number of WES workers in union jobs was relatively high. Second, the proportion of women who reported that the number of hours they worked per week changed "a lot" or "a fair amount" declined from 30 percent of those employed in 1997 to less than 18 percent in 2003. Stable hours are important for mothers who need to arrange child care as well as for low-wage workers for whom reduced earnings could lead to economic hardship. Likewise, more women obtained jobs with regular starting and ending times. In 1997, nearly 37 percent of employed respondents said that these times varied, whereas in 2003 this was true for 28 percent of workers.

There are numerous debates as to whether or not temporary employment is good or bad for low-skilled workers. As Autor and Houseman (2005) note, because employers do not have to make a long-term commitment to a temporary worker, they may be more willing to hire people, for example, welfare recipients, who would otherwise have a difficult time securing employment. Once hired, these individuals accumulate skills and work experience, which might help them secure other, more permanent, jobs. On the other hand, employers might be less willing to invest in building the skills of workers hired solely to fill some limited need. Also, such jobs rarely offer benefits and may only provide short-term employment. While temporary employment was not initially uncommon among working WES sample members—about a fifth of such women were "temp" workers in 1998—the proportion in these types of jobs dropped to 8 percent in 2003.

Improvements were also seen on other dimensions of a job that are important when considering employment advancement. Paid sick or vacation days and the ability to have health and retirement benefits signal that a job is higher up the employment ladder. Additionally, for women with young children, the opportunity to use a vacation or sick day when a child is ill and home from school may help maintain employment and contribute to advancement through the accumulation of stable work experience.

Table 2.4 shows that the proportion of workers whose employers offered paid sick days, paid vacation days, health plans, and retirement benefits all increased over the six-year study period. In all cases, the peak coverage was in 2001. In 2001, for example, about half of workers had jobs offering paid sick days, 63 percent had vacation benefits, close to two-thirds were offered health benefits, and more than half were offered retirement benefits. However, those proportions fell by about 5 to 8 percentage points between 2001 and 2003. In some cases, this is due to job changes. For example, among workers who reported that their employers offered vacation or sick days in 2001 but not in 2003, about three-fifths had switched jobs. Likewise, about half of workers who were offered employer-sponsored health insurance in 2001 but not in 2003 had moved into a different job. However, this still means that between one-half and two-fifths of the benefit loss between 2001 and 2003 occurred to women working in the same job. Additionally, availability does not always translate into take-up of a benefit. In 2003,

Table 2.4 Proportion of Working WES Respondents in Jobs with Various Characteristics

Characteristic	1997	1998	1999	2001	2003
Covered by union	10.8	12.0	15.4	17.3	16.6
Temporary position	—	20.0	16.6	10.4	7.7
Changing working hours	29.3	22.6	21.2	21.2	17.8
Regular start/end times	36.9	35.4	26.0	25.4	28.0
Sick days[a]	29.1	46.8	44.7	50.3	45.9
Vacation[a]	46.5	58.1	59.9	62.7	57.3
Health[a]	40.3	53.8	57.8	63.0	55.4
Retirement[a]	29.9	39.8	45.9	51.3	43.0

NOTE: The years shown represent the five survey periods. Questions about temporary jobs were not asked in 1997.
[a] Immediately or after a trial period.
SOURCE: Author's tabulations from WES data.

among those whose employers offered health insurance, just over half took this option, while 35 percent reported receiving Medicaid, and the remaining 14 percent were uninsured.

It is likely that the recession of 2001, which continues to affect Michigan's economy, played a role in the declining quality of employment, both for those who stayed in the same position and those who switched jobs. While the state's economy soared during the late 1990s, news accounts describing the economic situation in the early part of the next decade used terms such as faltering, sputtering, and ailing to portray the climate. The Ford Motor Company and General Motors, after doing well in the late 1990s, faced increased competition and rising labor costs, which contributed to both receiving a "junk" credit rating for their bonds in 2005 (Schneider 2005). Job losses in auto production spilled over into the entire manufacturing sector. In the nation as a whole, unemployment rates rose from about 4 percent in 2000 to 6 percent in 2003. Michigan's unemployment rate in 2000 was slightly lower than the national average, at 3.7 percent. However, in 2003, the state had one of the highest unemployment rates in the country, 7.1 percent (U.S. Department of Labor 2008b).

Some respondents lost their jobs or otherwise exited the labor force, with monthly employment rates dropping from about 75 to 80 percent of the sample in 2000 to around 70 percent in 2001 and onward. This decline in employment was not as great as might be expected, given the change in economic conditions. Further, despite the mixed picture that emerges when examining trends in employment attributes and wages, a single mother and her two children would have had pretax earnings above the poverty line, assuming full-time, full-year work at the median wage earned in 2003 ($8.35 an hour for the sample). On the other hand, the assumption of full-time and full-year work is not the reality for the average woman in the sample. For example, in 2003, the average women in our sample worked in about 8 of the 12 months; only 37.8 percent of the sample worked full time, full year in 2003 (Figure 2.3).

Over time, a small, but growing, proportion of WES respondents went without earnings from employment and without cash assistance. Turner, Danziger, and Seefeldt (2006) find that 9.1 percent of respondents were without work and cash welfare for at least 25 percent of the 79 months covered by the study. In addition to being without work and

Figure 2.3 Number of Months Worked among WES Workers

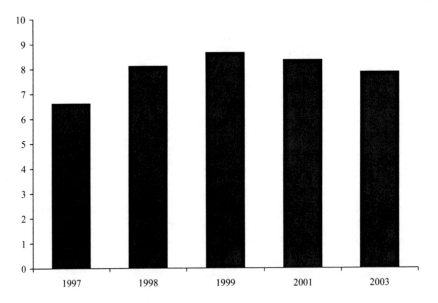

NOTE: The years shown represent the five survey periods.
SOURCE: Author's tabulations from WES data.

welfare for at least 20 months, they had no other earners in their households in at least three of the five years in which they were interviewed.

Among all respondents in fall 2003, 41.8 percent lived in households with gross income below the federal poverty line (Figure 2.4). If we take into account expenses, such as child care and transportation costs, 50.6 percent had monthly incomes below the poverty line. Thus, the conclusions that emerge from the WES are rather mixed. Contrary to the expectations of many who opposed the 1996 welfare reform, large numbers of recipients exited the rolls for work. Over time, some women moved into better-paying jobs with benefits, stable hours, and regular work schedules. However, others did not. In the next chapter, I explore personal and family challenges associated with various employment trajectories.

Figure 2.4 Proportion of WES Respondents with Household Income below the Poverty Line, 1997–2003

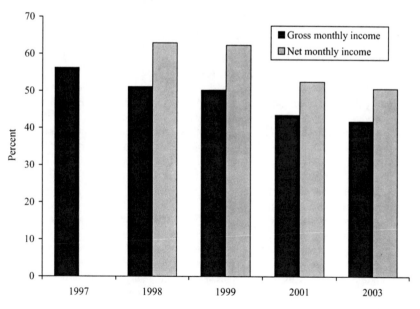

NOTE: The years shown represent the five survey periods. There was no net monthly income measure for 1997.

SOURCE: Author's tabulations from WES data.

Notes

1. Sandra Danziger, a sociologist, is the principal investigator of the WES. Key collaborators on the study include Mary Corcoran, an economist, Sheldon Danziger, an economist, Ariel Kalil, a developmental psychologist, and Richard Tolman, a social worker.
2. Although all women in our study were heads of single-parent cases, this does not necessarily mean that all were single mothers. For example, it was possible for a married-couple family to receive welfare as a single-parent case if one parent was disabled and received support through the Supplemental Security Income (SSI) program. The other parent and the children, if they qualified, could then receive welfare benefits.
3. The caseload in this county was such that there were too few recipients to study the experiences of members of other racial/ethnic groups or of noncitizens.
4. Although the WES was administered in one Michigan county, trends in the receipt of cash assistance and employment among WES recipients are quite similar to those of a national sample of welfare recipients drawn from the Survey of Income and Program Participation (SIPP). We drew a sample of all 853 single-mother welfare recipients from the 1996 SIPP panel who had the same age range as the WES sample (this analysis uses the WES wave 4-2001-sample, $n = 577$). At the start of both the WES and SIPP panels, 100 percent received cash welfare; by February 2000, 21.5 percent of WES and 31 percent of SIPP respondents were still receiving cash assistance. At the start of the panel, 42 percent of WES respondents and 35 percent of SIPP respondents were employed. Fifty-one months later, 71 percent of WES and 51 percent of SIPP respondents reported working. When we restrict the SIPP panel to African Americans and whites, we find that SIPP welfare recipients are roughly the same age (31.8 years old compared to 29.9 for WES), have similar household sizes (3.8 for SIPP and 3.9 for WES at the start of the panel), and are about as likely to have not completed high school (33.5 percent for SIPP and 29.3 percent for WES). On the other hand, WES respondents are more likely to be African American, even when the SIPP sample is restricted to only African Americans and whites (55.8 percent of WES respondents are African American versus 42.4 percent in SIPP).
5. Thirty-three women moved from TANF to SSI during the course of the study. Unless otherwise noted, these women are excluded from the analyses.
6. Monthly employment rates are based upon respondents' self-report as to whether or not they were working in a given month.
7. Figures derived by using the "Marriage Calculator" available from the Administration for Children and Families of the U.S. Department of Health and Human Services (2006).
8. Although this screener was administered in 2001, we use it as a baseline measure of a learning disability, since it is unlikely that a learning problem would have developed in the 1997–2001 period.
9. Respondents were asked to evaluate their health as excellent, very good, good,

fair, or poor. Questions on physical functioning come from the SF-36 Health Survey (Ware 1993), which asks about the extent to which respondents are limited in doing activities of everyday life, including lifting groceries, walking up stairs, sitting or standing, and the like. The resulting score is adjusted for a respondent's age.

3
Up the Ladder, Down the Ladder, or Stuck on the Same Rung?

In the mid-1980s, a community-based employment program called Project Match started working with residents of one of Chicago's infamous public housing developments, Cabrini Green, to help them find jobs. Project Match staff quickly realized that they could place many participants into jobs, but the greater challenge lay in helping people maintain employment and advance into higher-paying positions. Project Match developed the concept of the "Incremental Ladder to Economic Independence," which posited that moving from welfare to work was a process. For example, some individuals would need to start by doing volunteer work and acquiring soft skills, such as punctuality; others would combine part-time, minimum wage work with GED classes to develop greater human capital; while still others might be in various combinations of these and additional activities. The ultimate goal, though, was to move everyone, at their own pace, up the various "rungs" of the ladder so that all participants would eventually be working full-time in better-paying jobs with benefits.

In this chapter, I use the ladder metaphor to examine descriptively patterns in wage growth and job advancement for WES respondents over the study period. As it became clear that many recipients could find employment, a question arose as to whether the individuals could keep these jobs or obtain ones paying higher wages. On one side, some argue that many welfare recipients have significant problems that, while not impeding them from getting a position, may lead to quick job loss or slow wage growth (King and Mueser 2005). Some of these challenges include low education levels and poor work histories; high levels of physical and mental health problems; and family difficulties, including domestic violence and health issues, such as those described in the previous chapter (Danziger et al. 2000; Kalil et. al. 1998).

Others speculate that attributes of the positions, or even the low-wage labor market itself, may impede advancement. Low-wage jobs are often characterized as routinized and unchallenging, providing few opportunities for workers to learn new skills that might help them progress. Declines in manufacturing jobs and unionization and an increase in service sector employment have been cited as factors contributing to fewer opportunities for low-skilled workers to acquire better-paying employment (Danziger and Gottschalk 1995; Wilson 1996).

The WES data do not allow me to analyze the effects of macroeconomic changes on the employment advancement opportunities for welfare recipients. However, the rich data on personal and family characteristics enabled an examination of the extent to which some of the challenges faced by welfare recipients affect their employment trajectories. This work is similar to that undertaken by my colleagues, Rucker Johnson and Mary Corcoran. However, Johnson and Corcoran (2003) focus primarily on how the attributes of the jobs in which women worked (such as the types of skills used and the wages offered) were associated with movement from a bad job (low wage, no health benefits) to a good job (higher wage with benefits).[1] They find that individuals who, on a daily basis, used reading, writing, or computer skills at work, or had some supervisory responsibilities, were more likely to move from a bad job to a good job. People who worked in situations that involved serving customers, a task required by many service sector jobs, were significantly less likely to make this transition.

In the analyses presented in this chapter, the WES survey data are used to present a number of findings related to employment advancement. First, I consider growth in wages over time among those who were working at both the beginning and end of the study. After providing those descriptive results, I present a multivariate analysis to examine the role of personal characteristics (rather than the skill level of the jobs as Johnson and Corcoran do) on various employment pathways.

WAGE GROWTH DURING THE STUDY

The most uncomplicated way to examine wage growth over time is to compare respondents' wages at the start of the study to those at the end. Each time a WES respondent was interviewed, she was asked about the wage rate of her current job. If she was not working when the survey was conducted, she was asked about her most recent job, including the date when she last worked. I define the beginning wage as either the wage reported at the Fall 1997 interview (wave 1), the wage reported at the Fall 1998 (wave 2) interview if the respondent was not working at wave 1, or the wage of the most recent job in 1997 or 1998 if the respondent was not working when the interviewer conducted the 1997 and 1998 surveys. I define the ending wage as the wage reported for the most recent job in 2003, either the current job at the wave 5 interview or the most recent job during that calendar year.

Although this method uses several different starting dates for the initial wage, it provides more cases to analyze and is probably more representative of the wages sample members were able to obtain in the period shortly after welfare reform. Limiting the inquiry to just those women who were in jobs at the first interview might introduce bias into the results, since women who were the first to obtain jobs post-reform might have been the most employable and therefore might have earned higher wages than those who got jobs slightly later. Additionally, unstable employment patterns are not uncommon among low-skilled workers (Holzer and LaLonde 2000; Johnson and Corcoran 2003; Royalty 1998). Restricting this analysis to women working at a particular point in time (i.e., the month in which they were interviewed for this study) would miss individuals who had recently been working and had lost jobs, or who were between jobs.

Using these definitions, the sample includes 329 women, or 61 percent of the wave 5 sample, who have wage information for both periods.[2] Because I only included sample members who were employed some time at the beginning and end of the study, the women in this analysis are not representative of the sample as a whole. In particular, these 329 women worked in more months—about 80 percent of the 79 months in which the study observed them—whereas the average among the entire sample is 68 percent. To the extent that wage growth is correlated with steady employment, any results from this particular analysis will be upwardly biased.

Tables 3.1 and 3.2 provide descriptive information about the wages of these 329 women, expressed in 2003 dollars. As the first column of Table 3.1 shows, 53 percent earned less than $7 an hour in 1997, while 11.9 percent worked at jobs paying less than $5 an hour. Some women reporting wages less than the federal minimum wage worked in restaurants or bars, and thus their wages were lower because of an

Table 3.1 Characteristics of Initial and Ending Job for Those with Valid Starting and Ending Wages (n = 329)

	1997	2003
Hourly wages (in 2003 $)	%	
Less than $5.00	11.9	10.3
$5.00–$5.99	21.6	6.4
$6.00–$6.99	19.5	13.1
$7.00–$7.99	16.7	14.6
$8.00–$8.99	8.2	13.4
$9.00–$9.99	4.9	9.1
$10.00–$10.99	3.3	10.3
$11.00– $11.99	3.7	5.5
$12.00 or more	10.3	17.3
Median hourly wage	$6.78	$8.23
Usual hours worked per week	%	
1–19	9.1	4.9
20–34	41.6	28.0
35–40	33.1	51.7
More than 40	16.1	15.5
Average hours worked	33.0	36.4

NOTE: Columns may not total 100 due to rounding.
SOURCE: Author's tabulations from WES data.

expectation that they would be receiving tips. Other women worked in jobs subsidized by the state, such as child care providers or home health aides. Their wages were paid directly by the state Family Independence Agency (FIA, now called the Department of Human Services). Just under 30 percent had jobs paying in the $7 to $10 an hour range, 7 percent had wages between $10 and $12 an hour, and about 10 percent earned more than $12 an hour.

Inflation-adjusted wages increased modestly over the study period. For example, in 2003 about 16 percent of the women made between $10 and $12 an hour, compared to just 7 percent in 1997/1998, and more women, 17.3 percent, earned at least $12 an hour. The percentage of women earning less than $7 an hour fell from 53 to about 30 percent.

Table 3.2 Wage Growth Patterns, 1997/1998, for Those with Valid Starting and Ending Wages (*n* = 329)

	%
Percentage whose wages	
Increased	65.3
Decreased/stayed the same	34.7
Percentage change in wages	
More than 50%	29.2
26–50%	14.9
11–25%	11.6
0–10%	9.1
−1 to −10%	7.0
More than −10%	28.3
Change in real hourly wages (2003 $)	
More than $5.00	17.3
$2.50–$4.99	17.6
$1.00–$2.49	18.5
$0–$0.99	11.9
$0–$1.00	8.8
Loss of more than $1	25.8

NOTE: Columns may not total 100 due to rounding.
SOURCE: Author's tabulations from WES data.

The median hourly wage rose by about 21 percent, from $6.78 to $8.23. In addition to gains in the wage rate, the number of hours worked per week increased. In 1997, when part-time employment was more common, the average number of hours worked per week was 33, and just under half of the sample (49.2 percent) worked at least 35 hours a week. By 2003, 67.2 percent of respondents worked at least 35 hours each week, and mean hours had increased to over 36.

The overall distribution of wage rates does not tell us about individual trajectories. As Table 3.2 shows, 65.3 percent of respondents with valid wage information in both periods experienced an increase in real wages over time. Gains in real wages were substantial for some. Nearly 3 in 10 workers experienced more than a 50 percent increase in their hourly wage, while another 15 percent had wage increases between 26 and 50 percent. Nine percent had fairly negligible wage growth of 10 percent or less, and 7 percent had wage losses up to 10 percent. In adjusted dollar amounts, increases are fairly evenly distributed into raises of more than $5 an hour (17.3 percent), between $2.50 to $4.99 an hour (17.6 percent), and $1 to $2.49 an hour (18.5 percent), with a smaller group (11.9 percent) garnering an increase of less than a dollar an hour. Less than 10 percent of the analysis sample had *losses* between $0.01 and a dollar in real terms, but more than a quarter of workers saw their wages reduced in real terms by more than a dollar an hour.

EMPLOYMENT TRANSITIONS

While wage growth for some women was quite significant, it is important to remember that many individuals started off working in very low-paying jobs while others began the study earning more. Because of the variations in starting points, wage growth of the same percentage may have very different meanings for different women. For example, a woman who was earning $9 an hour in 1997 and experienced 25 percent growth in her wages would have been earning $11.25 in 2003. On the other hand, a minimum-wage ($5.15) worker in 1997 whose earnings subsequently grew 25 percent would only have been making $6.44 in 2003. Again, the information on wage growth presented earlier only considers women who had jobs at both the start and end of the WES and does not take into account the one-third of the sample working more sporadically or at least not in 1997, 1998, or 2003. Because unstable employment is so common, the remaining analyses attempt to look at the various employment pathways of a larger set of the sample.

Conceptualizing Employment Transitions

To address some of these issues, I grouped women into categories, based upon their hourly wage at the beginning and ending periods. Implicit in discussions of employment advancement and wage growth among former welfare recipients is an assumption that most of these workers are starting out on the bottom rungs of the labor market in jobs with very low pay. However, no clear definition of a "low-wage job" nor of a "low-wage worker" exists. In the United States the federal minimum wage, $5.15 an hour at the time the data were collected

(1997–2003), provides some guidance in that a general consensus exists that jobs paying within that range are probably "low wage." But how wide should the range be?

In other analyses of wage growth among low-wage workers, Schochet and Rangarajan (2004) and Andersson, Holzer, and Lane (2005) tie their definition of low wage to the federal poverty line. In the former case, the authors consider the amount an individual, working full time, full year would need to earn in order to put a family of four above the poverty line. Workers whose wages fall below that cutoff are considered to be in low-wage jobs. In the post-welfare reform period, this level would be about $7.50 an hour in 1996 and just over $8 in the early 2000s. A benefit of this method is that "low-wage" jobs are tied to a benchmark, namely the federal poverty line, which holds some meaning in the policy community.[3]

I roughly follow the categorization proposed by Schochet and Rangarajan (2004), whereby threshold hourly wages are computed based upon a woman's wage rate relative to the poverty line for a typical family.[4] For a family of *three* (a single mother and two children, the typical family in WES) and assuming full-time, full-year work, a sample member earning $6.15 an hour (or $6.25 in 1998) would have earnings putting her family below the federal poverty line. I consider these women to have "below-poverty-wage jobs" in the initial period. In 2003, the comparable wage rate for a below-poverty-wage job is $7.05 an hour.[5] I categorize women as having "above-poverty-wage jobs" if their hourly rate puts them above the federal poverty line. In 1997/1998 this would translate into wage rates above $6.16/6.26.[6]

These thresholds may strike some as rather low: $7.05 is only $1.90 over the federal minimum wage of $5.15. The cutoffs are tied to the official measurement of the poverty line, and some critics note that the poverty line calculation has not kept pace with changes in families' expenditures. The original definition assumed that families spent one-third of their income on food, and that premise still holds, despite evidence of significant changes in families' expenditure patterns. For example, families spend more of their income on housing and transportation and less on food (Economic Policy Institute 2001). Efforts to develop a measure that takes into account what a family requires to achieve a "basic" standard of living generally find that a family of four would need to make about $30,000 a year (Bernstein, Brocht, and

Spade-Aguilar 2000). Translated into an hourly wage, this is just over $14, substantially more than the amount I use to delineate low- from higher-wage workers.

Living wage ordinances require employers (although usually only those that contract with city or county government) to pay more than the federal minimum in an effort to help lower-wage workers; these rules are typically set at 100 to 130 percent of the poverty line (Economic Policy Institute 2006). Milwaukee, another midwestern city, has a minimum living wage of $6.25. The threshold that I use, then, matches well to what some consider living wages, albeit very conservative ones.

For lower-wage workers, some income will likely come from sources other than wages. For example, many will qualify for food stamps. Although eligibility for the program is in part tied to income and earnings, the cutoff is higher than it is for the Temporary Assistance to Needy Families (TANF) program. Of course, not all low-wage workers are eligible for the program, and not all eligible families participate. However, the typical single mother of two in our Michigan sample, who works at a job paying $7.05 an hour, could expect to get about $220 a month in food stamps. Additionally, low-wage workers' income has been greatly boosted by expansions to the Earned Income Tax Credit (EITC). The EITC is a refundable tax credit, designed in part to reduce the regressiveness of payroll taxes or other income taxes. The amount of the credit received is contingent upon work and earnings levels. The credit rises with earnings, peaking at around $4,400 (in 2005) for single-parent workers with two or more children earning between $11,000 and $14,400 a year. At income levels higher than that, the amount of the credit declines, phasing out entirely at just over $35,000 a year. A typical WES respondent working at the poverty threshold wage rate of $7.05 might have received more than $3,000 in EITC payments. Assuming she worked full time, full year at this rate, received food stamps and the EITC, her income, net of payroll and state income taxes, would have been more than $20,000, or about 130 percent of the federal poverty line that year.[7]

Transitions in and out of Poverty-Wage Jobs

Among respondents working in 1997 or 1998, 55.1 percent were in poverty-wage jobs and 44.9 percent earned above the poverty wage.

By 2003, a much smaller proportion, 26.6 percent, were in poverty-wage positions, with 50.8 percent earning higher pay. The remaining 22.6 percent reported no work during calendar year 2003, and thus I categorize them as being unemployed.[8] Of course, these proportions are computed for those who worked at the start of the study. Although the sample size for this analysis, 421 women, is larger than the sample used in the beginning of the chapter ($n = 329$) to look at wage growth, 115 of the 536 wave 5 respondents, or 21 percent, are still excluded.

However, any analysis of employment transitions needs information on wage rates for at least some roughly comparable time period. The excluded cases had very limited employment over the entire WES study time frame and not enough wage information to classify them for these analyses. This group worked in only 37 percent of the months, or about 29 of the 79 months we followed them. About 20 percent of this group had moved onto the rolls of the SSI program, the federal disability program for low-income individuals. As such, they were not expected to work. Another 20 percent were married and perhaps worked less because their husbands earned enough money to support their families. On the other hand, while the group excluded from the analysis received welfare in more of the months as compared to those included (35 percent of months versus 19 percent of months), some of those we dropped are likely part of a group whom many researchers refer to as the "disconnected." (For example, see Loprest [2002]; Turner, Danziger, and Seefeldt [2006]; and Wood and Rangarajan [2003].) That is, they have no income from work, no cash assistance from welfare, and, in some cases, no support from other adult earners. While the problems faced by this group have recently received a great deal of attention from researchers and policymakers, they are not the focus of this analysis.

Table 3.3 examines those with valid starting wages ($n = 421$) and displays the employment transition matrix. About 17 percent started in a poverty-wage job and ended in one; 24.7 percent started in a poverty-wage job and moved into a higher-paying position. Thirteen percent of those working at the start were not employed in the 12 months prior to the 2003 interview. About a quarter of workers, 26.1 percent, both began and ended in jobs paying above-poverty wages. Just under a tenth (9.3 percent) moved from above-poverty wages to a poverty-level job. A similar proportion worked in jobs with above-poverty wages at the start of the study but were not employed at all in 2003.

Table 3.3 Employment Transitions, 1997/1998 to 2003, for Workers with Valid Starting Wages (*n* = 421)

Transition type	%	Median hourly wage in 2003
Poverty wage both periods	17.3	$6.00
Poverty wage to above-poverty wage	24.7	$9.00
Poverty wage to unemployment	13.1	n/a
Above-poverty wage both periods	26.1	$10.50
Above-poverty wage to poverty wage	9.3	$5.89
Above-poverty wage to unemployment	9.5	n/a

NOTE: A poverty-wage job is equivalent to $6.15 an hour or less in 1997 and $7.05 an hour or less in 2003.
SOURCE: Author's tabulations from WES data.

PERSONAL CHARACTERISTICS AND THE RELATIONSHIP TO EMPLOYMENT TRANSITIONS

A few other studies have examined the association between personal characteristics and employment transitions among welfare recipients. For example, Pavetti and Acs (1997) use data from the National Longitudinal Survey of Youth (NLSY) and calculate the probability that women moved into a "good job," defined as working 35 hours a week and earning at least $8 per hour (in 1993 dollars). Less than half, 47.4 percent, of women who did not complete high school ever worked in a good job, as opposed to about two-thirds of women with high school diplomas. Loeb and Corcoran (2001), though, also using the NLSY, find no difference in wage growth between AFDC recipients and women who were not recipients, controlling for work experience. Assuming full-time employment, their analyses indicate that women could expect wage growth of about 6 percent a year. Any differences in actual wage growth, they contend, are due to the lower levels of work by welfare recipients, who, at that time, were more likely to be employed part time and sporadically over the course of a year.

However, this work with the NLSY was conducted under the previous welfare system, AFDC, which had far fewer employment requirements. Additionally, the data sets used in many prior studies contain limited information on personal characteristics. For example, Pavetti and Acs were only able to control for six demographic variables: age, race, marital status, educational attainment, number of children, and age of youngest child. Loeb and Corcoran control for similar characteristics and add in previous work experience and a measure of cognitive ability, the test score on the Air Force Qualifying Test (AFQT). In their study, Schochet and Rangarajan (2004), whose general approach I follow, had access to a measure of self-reported health limitations but no information on mental health problems, detailed work experience measures, or experiences with domestic violence, all of which may affect advancement prospects. With the WES, I am able to examine some of these relationships.

WES Measures

The WES contains extensive indicators of personal and family characteristics that might affect women's ability to move into, or get and keep, higher-paying jobs. In addition to basic demographic information (age, race, marital status, and number of children living in the household), the study includes details concerning respondents' human capital. Respondents are categorized by whether they had less than a high school diploma or no GED, a high school diploma or GED, or additional schooling beyond high school. Also included is an indicator of potential learning disabilities, a measure of "low" work experience, and a descriptor of skills used on previous jobs. The last element is based on Harry Holzer's work on employers in the low-wage labor market. Holzer surveyed employers in four cities whose firms hired at least some workers without college degrees. He found that, even for some jobs that might be labeled "low skill," employers required their new hires to have completed high school as well as to have had work experience. In part this may be because many of these jobs required their holders to use at least some cognitive skills, including reading and writing paragraphs, doing arithmetic, and using computers (Holzer 1996). The Holzer "skill" variable measures whether or not a respondent had previously worked in a job that required her to use some of these proficiencies. Other human capital variables in the WES are the work norms barrier that the WES team developed (e.g., the respondent does not understand that being on time, not talking back to a supervisor, and coming into work are important qualities in an employee) and a measure capturing instances of prior workplace discrimination (refer to Chapter 2 for more details on all of these measures).

With the exception of education, all of the human capital variables were measured at baseline, 1997, or in the case of the learning disability, 2001. These baseline measures, as opposed to those collected in later survey waves, are not affected by subsequent employment. For example, the more one works, the greater experience one acquires, or the increased opportunity one has to use more skills or to be exposed to workplace discrimination. The 1997 measures are a close approximation to the effect of the barrier on employment, rather than the other way around. The employment barrier measures are categorized by the duration over which a woman reported them. I took advantage of the panel nature of the WES data and included measures for the presence of other characteristics over time. Following the convention used by my colleagues Corcoran, Danziger, and Tolman (2004), I coded the employment barrier variables to represent whether a respondent had the particular barrier at one or two survey waves or three or more waves; never having the barrier is the omitted category. Additionally, I included variables that measured whether or not the respondent was married at none, one or two, or three or more survey waves; and whether or not the number of children in her household increased from baseline (continuing to control for the number of children present at baseline).

The rationale for including measures of the duration of the employment barriers is that having a certain problem at baseline might not necessarily have a great effect on an individual's cumulative employment, but the continued presence of that barrier might. For example, women who were depressed once in 1997 might experience some job instability at that time, but once over the illness, resume working with limited impact experienced on their overall employment trajectory. Similarly, women who return to school and acquire more education might be able to overcome any deficits that a lack of a high school diploma might initially have on their employment and thus get on a better trajectory. Women who have only two children at baseline and no others throughout the period might have better employment outcomes than similar women who have additional children and take time out of the labor market. Thus, controlling only for baseline characteristics might miss some of the other factors that could contribute to being on various employment pathways. Details about all of these measures are provided in Appendix A.

Construction of Multivariate Analyses

In order to look at the various transition patterns, I divided the sample into those who had started out working in poverty-wage jobs and those who began in above-poverty-wage jobs, since it is very likely that these two groups are different in their characteristics.[9] Within those two segments, I further divided the sample into 1) those who ended the study period in a poverty-wage job, 2) those who ended in an above-poverty-wage job, and 3) those who were unemployed in 2003. Among all women starting in a poverty-wage job ($n = 232$), 73 remained in this type of job in 2003, 104 had moved to a better-paying position, while the remaining 55 were unemployed (Table A.1). Among women starting in an above-poverty-wage job ($n = 189$), 39 moved into a poverty-wage job by 2003, 110 remained in better-paying employment, and 40 were unemployed (Table A.2). I refer to all of these categorizations as "employment transition groups."

The goal of the analyses is to determine which personal and family characteristics are associated with various transition patterns. Table 3.4 lists all of the variables included in the regressions and provides brief definitions and the time when the characteristic was measured. Appendix A provides the descriptive statistics for all of the variables as well as more details on the multivariate models used, including regression coefficients and standard errors.

The remainder of this chapter presents the results of the analyses and my interpretations of those findings. Because of the nature of the model used in this analysis, these transitions will be reported relative to some other situation. That is, one variable might be associated with an increase in the odds of moving into a better-paying opportunity, relative to remaining in a poverty-wage job, while another variable may be linked to increased odds of staying in a poverty-wage job relative to becoming unemployed.[10] To avoid confusion, I consider each transition separately.

I use a multinomial regression model, the results of which can be difficult to interpret (since the coefficients represent logged odds). As an alternative, I present predicted probabilities. In statistical terms, the

Table 3.4 Variables Used in Multivariate Analyses

Variable	Definition	Year(s) measured
Race	Dummy variable equal to 1 if respondent is African American (0 = white)	1997
Age	Three dummy variables of ranges 18–24 (omitted), 25–34, 35 or older	1997
Number of children	Number of minor-aged, care-given children living with the respondent	1997
Increase in number of children	Dummy variable indicating that the number of children in the household in 2003 was greater than the number in 1997	2003
Married	Three sets of dummy variables indicating whether the respondent was married in 1) one or two of the survey waves or 2) three or more of the survey waves. Never married in any survey wave is the omitted category.	Constructed using information from all survey waves
Education	Three dummy variables indicating that the respondent has 1) no high school diploma or GED, 2) a high school diploma or GED—the omitted category, or 3) education beyond high school	2003
Work norms barrier	Dummy variable indicating that the respondent did not know five of nine workplace norms	1997
Low work experience	Dummy variable indicating that the respondent had worked in less than 20 percent of the months as an adult	1997
Work skills barrier	Dummy variable indicating that the respondent had performed fewer than four skill types in previous jobs	1997
Learning disability	Dummy variable indicating that the respondent scored at or below the 5th grade level on a reading test	1999
Prior discrimination	Dummy variable indicating that the respondent reported at least one incidence of workplace discrimination based on race, gender, and/or welfare status	1997

Variable	Description	Notes
Transportation barrier	Three dummy variables indicating that a respondent lacked a driver's license and/or access to a car in 1) no survey waves—omitted category, 2) one or two survey waves, or 3) three or more survey waves	Constructed using information from all survey waves
Mental health problem	Three dummy variables indicating that a respondent met the diagnostic screening criteria for any mental health disorder in 1) no survey waves—omitted category, 2) one or two survey waves, or 3) three or more survey waves. The disorders considered are major depression, generalized anxiety disorder, posttraumatic stress disorder, social phobia, and alcohol dependence	Constructed using information from all survey waves
Physical health problem	Three dummy variables indicating that a respondent considered her health "fair" or "poor" *and* she scored in the lowest quartile for a variety of physical functioning tasks in 1) no survey waves—omitted category, 2) one or two survey waves, or 3) three or more survey waves.	Constructed using information from all survey waves
Child health problem	Three dummy variables indicating that at least one child had a physical or emotional problem that interfered with the respondent's ability to work in 1) no survey waves—omitted category, 2) one or two survey waves, or 3) three or more survey waves	Constructed using information from all survey waves
Drug use	Three dummy variables indicating that a respondent reported using illicit drugs in 1) no survey waves—omitted category, 2) one or two survey waves, or 3) three or more survey waves	Constructed using information from all survey waves
Domestic violence	Three dummy variables indicating that a respondent experienced severe partner abuse in 1) no survey waves—omitted category, 2) one or two survey waves, or 3) three or more survey waves	Constructed using information from all survey waves

predicted probabilities approximate the marginal effects of the significant variables. In more straightforward language, the predicted probability can be thought of as the change in the probability that a woman will make one of the various employment transitions, given a change in one of her characteristics. For example, assume that a particular woman starting the study in a poverty-wage job also had the work skills barrier in 1997. In this example, the probability that she will move into an above-poverty-wage job is 73.7 percent. Without the skills barrier, the probability of moving into an above-poverty-wage job falls to 62.7 percent (see Figure 3.1).

In order to produce the predicted probabilities, I use the characteristics of the "modal" or typical WES survey respondent who was working in a poverty-wage job in 1997/1998 and of the typical respondent who was working in an above-poverty-wage job at that same time.[11] I then vary each significant characteristic, one at a time, to see how much the probability of making a particular transition is influenced by the characteristic (see Figures 3.1–3.6 and Appendix A for more details). The modal respondent starting in a poverty-wage job had a 14.6 percent likelihood of being in a poverty-wage job in 2003, a 62.7 percent likelihood of moving into a higher-paying position, and a 22.7 percent likelihood of becoming unemployed. Similarly, by 2003 the typical respondent starting in an above-poverty-wage job had a 9.4 percent likelihood of making a downward transition to a poverty-wage job, an 86.9 percent likelihood of staying in an above-poverty-wage job, and a 3.8 percent likelihood of being unemployed.

EMPLOYMENT TRANSITIONS FROM POVERTY-WAGE JOBS

Women who began the study working in poverty-wage jobs might have been working at this level at the end of the period, they might have moved into higher-paying positions, or they might have ended the study unemployed.

Figure 3.1 Predicted Probabilities of Ending in an Above-Poverty-Wage Job among WES Respondents Starting in a Poverty-Wage Job, Significant Factors

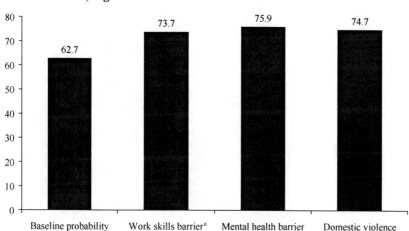

NOTE: The baseline probability is for the "modal" respondent who never had any employment barriers during the study. Please refer to Note 11 for further information on the modal respondent. Refer to Table 3.4 for definitions of the measures.
[a] The change in the predicted probability is relative to becoming unemployed.
[b] The change in the predicted probability is relative to staying in a poverty-wage job.
SOURCE: Author's tabulations from WES data.

Remaining in Poverty-Wage Jobs

A number of factors were significantly associated with being in poverty-wage jobs about six years later. First, women with larger families in 1997 were more likely to be in a poverty-wage job in 2003 as opposed to moving up the economic ladder. If the typical respondent starting in a poverty-wage job had three children instead of two, her probability of remaining in a poverty-wage job in 2003 would have been 18.6 percent, a 4-percentage-point increase over the baseline probability of 14.6 percent (Figure 3.2). Women with larger families may be relegated to very low-wage jobs if the positions that pay better are less flexible in regard to scheduling. Having more children often means greater challenges with securing child care, particularly if that care is with different providers.

Figure 3.2 Predicted Probabilities of Ending in a Poverty-Wage Job among WES Respondents Starting in a Poverty-Wage Job, Significant Factors

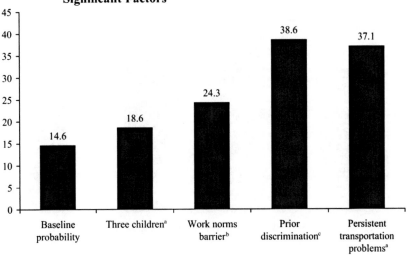

NOTE: The baseline probability is for the "modal" respondent who never had any employment barriers during the study. Please refer to Note 11 for further information on the modal respondent. Refer to Table 3.4 for definitions of the measures.
[a] The change in the predicted probability is relative to moving into an above-poverty-wage job.
[b] The change in the predicted probability is relative to becoming unemployed.
[c] The change in the predicted probability is relative to moving into an above-poverty-wage job and to becoming unemployed.
SOURCE: Author's tabulations from WES data.

Not knowing appropriate workplace norms increased the probability of remaining employed in a poverty-wage job relative to becoming unemployed. If the typical respondent had the workplace norms barrier, the probability that she would remain in a poverty-wage job increased to 24.3 percent. This finding runs counter to what the literature would have predicted. One might assume that not knowing proper workplace behavior would be associated with job loss, since employers might be unlikely to tolerate lateness and absenteeism. However, over time, workers may have come to learn the importance of various work norms, and thus having this barrier early in one's career may not matter in the longer run.

Having previously experienced discrimination in the workplace increased the probability of staying in a poverty-wage job, relative both to moving up the ladder and to later unemployment. The change in the probability of remaining on the lower rung of the employment ladder associated with having this barrier is fairly large: an increase from 14.6 to 38.6 percent. Women who experience discrimination may feel discouraged about their prospects for obtaining better jobs and not seek them out (although it may not affect their ability to get a job).

Having persistent transportation problems over the course of the study period increased the probability of remaining in a poverty-wage job, relative to advancing. For the typical WES respondent, prolonged transportation problems were associated with an increase in the probability of staying in a poverty-wage job of 22.5 percentage points, up to 37.1 percent. Women with transportation problems may have constrained job choices and may stay in poverty-wage positions because they lack the ability to travel to search for better opportunities, or, if such jobs are located farther from their homes, to commute.

Moving to Above-Poverty-Wage Jobs

Several characteristics are associated with the transition into an above-poverty-wage job, although it is difficult to determine how these relationships work. For example, having the "Holzer work skills barrier" is associated with an increase in the probability of moving into an above-poverty-wage job, as opposed to becoming unemployed. If a poverty-wage worker in 1997/1998 had this barrier, her probability of going into an above-poverty-wage job increased from 62.7 to 73.7 percent (Figure 3.2). Similarly, having a mental health problem in one or two survey waves is associated with an increase in the probability of moving into an above-poverty-wage job, relative to becoming unemployed, of 13.2 percentage points (from 62.7 to 75.9 percent). Finally, among those starting in a poverty-wage job, experiences of severe abuse reported in one or two survey waves are associated with an increase in the probability of moving to above-poverty-wage jobs, relative to staying in a poverty-wage job.

All of these findings are puzzling, since they indicate that the presence of certain problems or barriers, at least at some point during the study, facilitates movement into higher-paying jobs. Perhaps the timing of some of these difficulties, which is not captured in this model, matters. That is, if mental health problems and domestic violence occurred earlier in the study period, then maybe these transitions are plausible.

Becoming Unemployed

Among those starting off in poverty-wage jobs, lack of work experience is associated with subsequent unemployment in 2003, relative both to continued poverty-wage employment and to an upward transition. This effect is also very large, increasing the probability of being unemployed from 22.7 up to 73.7 percent (Figure 3.3). While the strong economy in the late 1990s may have helped women with little work experience get an initial job, the cooldown that followed may have resulted in women with limited experience losing those jobs and having more difficulty finding new ones.

Persistent transportation problems (in three or more waves) increased the probability of becoming unemployed relative to staying in a poverty-wage job. The effect of having this barrier raised the likelihood of unemployment for the modal respondent by 9 percentage points. Likewise, having a physical health problem in at least three waves increased the probability of becoming unemployed relative to staying employed (either in a poverty- or above-poverty-wage job). This effect is also large, increasing the probability of unemployment in 2003 from 22.7 percent to 74.7 percent.

It is not hard to imagine that women who consistently had difficulties with transportation would be unemployed in 2003. Lack of transportation has long been recognized as a barrier to finding and keeping jobs. Women who had persistent health problems also may have had trouble holding jobs, or their health problems may have prevented them from working at all. Alternatively, these women may have returned to welfare and have been exempted from the work requirement. In other analyses, we find that persistent health problems were associated with lengthy stays on welfare (Seefeldt and Orzol 2005). During the time that the WES was conducted, Michigan did not require women who had documented health problems, including those in the process of applying for disability through the SSI program, to meet the work requirements.

Figure 3.3 Predicted Probabilities of Becoming Unemployed among WES Respondents Starting in a Poverty-Wage Job, Significant Factors

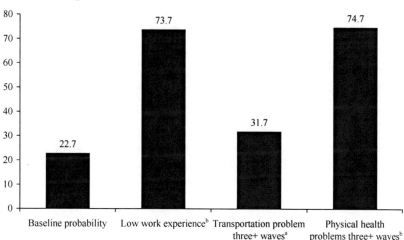

NOTE: The baseline probability is for the "modal" respondent who never had any employment barriers during the study. Please refer to Note 11 for further information on the modal respondent. Refer to Table 3.4 for definitions of the measures.
[a] The change in the predicted probability is relative to staying in a poverty-wage job.
[b] The change in the predicted probability is relative to remaining in a poverty-wage job and to moving into an above-poverty-wage job.
SOURCE: Author's tabulations from WES data.

EMPLOYMENT TRANSITIONS FROM ABOVE-POVERTY-WAGE JOBS

Again, women who started in the study working in above-poverty-wage positions had three possible outcomes at the end of the project: 1) moving down the economic ladder into a poverty-wage job, 2) remaining in an above-poverty-wage job, or 3) becoming unemployed.

Moving Down to Poverty-Wage Jobs

Among those starting in above-poverty-wage jobs, having more children increased the probability of a downward employment transition, both relative to staying in an above-poverty-wage job and relative to experiencing subsequent unemployment. While the effect on unemployment is not particularly large (Figure 3.6 displays a change in the predicted probability from 3.8 to 7.3 percent), having three children instead of two is associated with an increase in the probability of a downward transition of 7 percentage points (from 9.4 to 16.4 percent, as shown in Figure 3.4). Women with more children may find it difficult to stay on the higher rungs of the employment ladder if the jobs that pay better are more difficult to juggle with family demands.

Figure 3.4 Predicted Probabilities of Ending in a Poverty-Wage Job among WES Respondents Starting in an Above-Poverty-Wage Job, Significant Factors

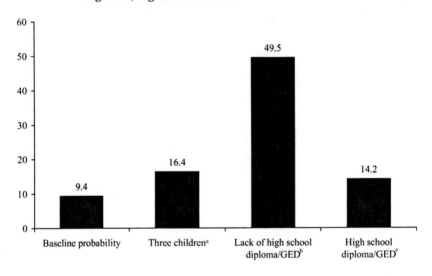

NOTE: The baseline probability is for the "modal" respondent who had a mental health problem in one or two survey waves. Please refer to Note 11 for more information on the modal respondent. Refer to Table 3.4 for definitions of the measures.
[a] The change in the predicted probability is relative to remaining in an above-poverty-wage job.
[b] The change in the predicted probability is relative to remaining in an above-poverty-wage job and to becoming unemployed.
[c] The change in predicted probability is relative to becoming unemployed.
SOURCE: Author's tabulations from WES data.

A lack of a high school diploma was significantly related to a downward employment transition, as opposed to maintaining an above-poverty-wage job or to becoming unemployed, and the effect is extremely large. If the typical WES respondent starting in an above-poverty-wage job had more than a high school education, her baseline probability of making a downward transition was 9.4 percent. If she instead did not have a high school diploma, the probability of ending up in a poverty-wage job in 2003 was 49.5 percent, a change of more than 40 percentage points.

In 1997 and 1998, the beginning years of the WES, the nation's economy was booming, and unemployment rates were at record lows. When I talked to Work First program managers, many contended that "anyone" could get a job and that employers were really only looking for someone who could show up to work on time—other skills or credentials mattered little. By 2003, the labor market was more competitive, particularly in Michigan. It could be that, while a lack of a high school diploma did not initially hinder some women from getting higher-paying jobs, in later years the positions available to them did not pay as well.

Remaining in an Above-Poverty-Wage Job

Being African American increased the probability of staying in a higher-paying job relative to becoming unemployed. If the typical respondent were white instead of African American, her probability of being unemployed in 2003 would have been approximately 9.1 percent, as opposed to 3.8 percent (Figure 3.6). Given the literature on employment discrimination among this population, I had predicted an opposite relationship (Kennelly 1999; Neckerman and Kirschenman 1991). I have no good explanation for this finding, other than to speculate that it is related to the characteristics of the study county, which has high rates of both white and African American poverty (as opposed to just concentrated African American poverty). Additionally, although statistically significant, the effect is not as substantially large as some others.

Surprisingly, having low work experience is associated with maintaining an above-poverty-wage position relative to moving into a poverty-wage job (an increase in the probability of remaining on a higher rung of the employment ladder from 86.9 to 91.9 percent, as seen in

Figure 3.5). However, as shown in the following discussion, low work experience also increases the probability of becoming unemployed, relative to remaining in an above-poverty-wage job, so this finding must be interpreted with caution. The strong economy, along with a "push" from the welfare office, might have contributed to women with limited experience getting a job in the late 1990s, even one that paid a higher wage. However, for some women, but perhaps not others, a lack of prior experience might have contributed to job loss and/or to their being less attractive to subsequent employers. Recall, too, that this variable was measured in 1997 and will not reflect actual work history by 2003.

Experiencing severe partner abuse in three to five of the survey waves was associated with continued employment in an above-poverty-wage job, relative to becoming unemployed (increasing the probability

Figure 3.5 Predicted Probabilities of Remaining in an Above-Poverty-Wage Job among WES Respondents Starting in an Above-Poverty-Wage Job, Significant Factors

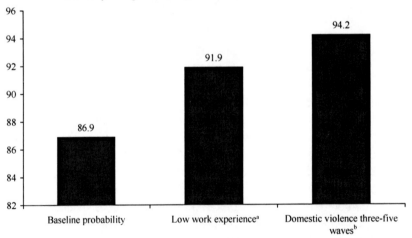

NOTE: The baseline probability is for the "modal" respondent who had a mental health problem in one or two survey waves. Please refer to Note 11 for more information on the modal respondent. Refer to Table 3.4 for definitions of the measures.
[a] The change in the predicted probability is relative to moving into a poverty-wage job.
[b] The change in the predicted probability is relative to moving into a below-poverty-wage job and to becoming unemployed.
SOURCE: Author's tabulations from WES data.

of remaining in an above-poverty-wage job from 86.9 percent to 94.2 percent). This is a puzzling result, given the prior literature on domestic violence and work. One of the ways in which partner abuse is theorized to interact with women's employment is through disruptions at work and control over decision making (Tolman and Raphael 2000). However, it could be that, for the women in our sample, partner abuse did not operate in this manner. Or, it could be that some women, after experiencing abuse, left the violent partners and sought better-paying jobs to ensure their economic security.

Figure 3.6 Predicted Probabilities of Becoming Unemployed among WES Respondents Starting in an Above-Poverty-Wage Job, Significant Factors

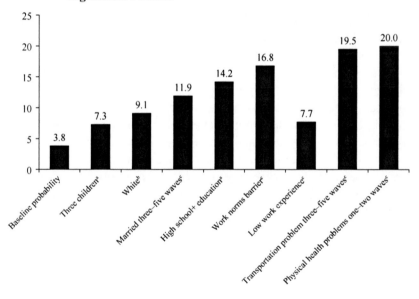

NOTE: The baseline probability is for the "modal" respondent who had a mental health problem in one or two survey waves. Please refer to Note 11 for more information on the modal respondent. Refer to Table 3.4 for definitions of the measures.
[a] The change in the predicted probability is relative to moving into a poverty-wage job.
[b] The change in the predicted probability is relative to remaining in an above-poverty-wage job.
[c] The change in the predicted probability is relative to staying in an above-poverty-wage job and to moving into a below-poverty-wage job.
SOURCE: Author's tabulations from WES data.

Becoming Unemployed

Among those starting in above-poverty-wage jobs, being married in the majority of the survey waves was associated with an increased probability of becoming unemployed by 2003. The effect is quite large: if a respondent was married most of the time instead of being single, the probability of her becoming unemployed would increase by more than 8 percentage points, from 3.8 to 11.9 percent (Figure 3.6). It could be that these exits from the labor market were not entirely involuntary. If married women's husbands earned good wages, then they may have decided not to work (or to work less). In other analyses, Danziger et al. (2002) found that the monthly earnings of adults living with WES respondents—typically their spouses or romantic partners—were, on average, $1,578, about a third higher than the average for women who worked. Women who have another earner in the household for longer periods of time may not feel the need to work, or, if they lose jobs, may take a longer time to find a new one.[12]

Having completed some education beyond high school increased the probability of becoming unemployed from an above-poverty-wage job, but only relative to moving into a poverty-wage job. Women with more education might have higher expectations for their jobs (including higher reservation wages) and, when faced with a job loss, may wait longer to find a higher-paying job as opposed to taking a lower-paying job. By contrast, if the typical respondent had exactly a high school diploma, the probability of transitioning into a poverty-wage job, relative to becoming unemployed, increased from 9.4 percent to 14.2 percent.

Not knowing appropriate workplace norms is associated with a transition from an above-poverty-wage job to later unemployment. The change in the probability associated with having this employment barrier is 13 percentage points (from 3.8 percent to 16.8 percent). Low prior work experience is also associated with unemployment, although the effect is not as large as observed among those starting in poverty-wage jobs. The probability of going from an above-poverty-wage job to being unemployed rises from 3.8 to 7.7 percent if the typical respondent had limited work experience in 1997. Similar to the findings about lack of work experience and low education levels, having these barriers may not have stopped women from securing better-paying jobs during the economic boom but may have prevented them from keeping these positions as the economy cooled.

For those starting in above-poverty-wage jobs, persistent transportation problems were associated with being unemployed in 2003, with an increase in the probability of job loss of almost 16 percentage points. Having a physical health problem in one to two waves increased the likelihood of becoming unemployed, relative to staying employed, and the effect is very large. The predicted probability of unemployment increases from 3.8 percent to 20 percent, an increase of 16.2 percentage points.

SUMMARY OF FINDINGS

This chapter has presented WES research findings related to wage growth and the association between personal and family characteristics and various employment transitions. I find that among those who worked fairly steadily (i.e., those who had valid wage information at both the start and end of the study), earnings growth was quite modest. In 2003 dollars, median wages increased from $6.78 an hour in 1997 and 1998 to $8.23 an hour in 2003. This represents an increase of just over 20 percent or about 3–4 percent per year, a fairly low rate, particularly given the wage at which the median worker started and that, for most of this period, the country was experiencing strong economic growth. Assuming full-time, full-year work (a very generous assumption, since only about half of workers were employed 12 months in 1998, rising to 70 percent in 2003), the median worker in 2003 would gross just over $17,000 in earnings.

Presenting changes in the median wage masks a great deal of heterogeneity within the sample. The 421 respondents who were working at the beginning of the study had varying employment trajectories, although even in the "best case" scenarios, wages remained fairly low. As shown in Table 3.3, over 17 percent of working sample members started and ended the study employed in "poverty-wage" jobs, or positions that paid less than $7.05 an hour (in 2003 dollars). Among these workers, though, the median wage received in 2003 was about $6 an hour, nearly a dollar an hour less than the cutoff used in these analyses. A smaller fraction, 9 percent, were working in "above-poverty-wage" jobs (i.e., jobs paying more than $7.05 an hour) when the study started, but by 2003 they were no longer being paid this much and instead were in poverty-wage jobs. The median hourly wage of this group in 2003 was $5.89. Additionally, more than one-fifth of those who were employed in 1997 or 1998 were not employed at all in 2003. While some of these women were married and relying on the income of their spouses and others might have been receiving disability payments, it is likely that some were also getting by on very little income and experiencing hardship (Turner, Danziger, and Seefeldt 2006).

Among those who had better employment trajectories in terms of their wages, pay growth was still quite modest. Referring back to Table 3.3, just under a quarter began the study employed in poverty-wage jobs but had moved into above-poverty-wage jobs by 2003. The median hourly wage of this group of individuals was $9, about a $2 hourly increase over their early wage, but still not enough to put a worker over $20,000 a year in earnings. Finally, even the group of women who had above-poverty-wage jobs at the beginning and end of the study were not, on average, earning very high wages; in 2003 the median hourly wage was $10.50.

The regression analyses provide clues as to some of the factors that could be associated with various employment trajectories. For example, a number of human capital problems, such as not knowing proper workplace behaviors, low levels of previous work experience, and prior discrimination, are associated with ending the study in a poverty-wage job or with unemployment. Likewise, persistent transportation problems and persistent health problems were significantly related to remaining in a poverty-wage job or to becoming unemployed. This set of findings suggests that the strong economy of the late 1990s allowed some women to get low-paying jobs but that they did not necessarily advance or enjoy stable employment.

These analyses provide some insight into the types of barriers that keep people in lower-paying jobs or contribute to unemployment. Yet, some of the barriers that have the largest effects on lack of mobility or on unemployment are ones that are fairly uncommon. For example, not knowing appropriate workplace norms is associated with later unemployment for those starting in above-poverty-wage jobs, while low work experience is associated with unemployment for those starting in poverty-wage jobs. But, as seen in Chapter 2, less than 10 percent of the sample did not know correct work behavior, and only 14 percent had low work experience. Furthermore, the analyses give little insight into the processes that might facilitate transitions into higher-wage jobs. In large part this is a result of the goal of the WES, which was to measure impediments to employment and the effects of those barriers.

Finally, even in instances for which one could make sensible guesses as to some of the possible explanations behind the associations that have been presented, the multivariate results are only that, associations. For example, it is reasonable to surmise that women with more children might have greater difficulties finding or arranging child care and thus might be more prone to experiencing downward employment transitions; however, we do not know definitively that child care challenges are what lie behind this finding. In order to gain insight into some of the processes around employment transitions and, more specifically, the decisions women make about which jobs to take when, I turn to a discussion of the qualitative data collected from a subsample of WES participants.

The next several chapters will use information from the qualitative supplement of the WES to illustrate some of the employment patterns that have been described. The career trajectories of these women reflect, in general, those of the entire sample; many moved up the employment ladder, a few moved down, and some were stuck on the same rung. However, through in-depth discussions we were able to learn more about the problems the women encountered in finding and keeping jobs and the choices and trade-offs they made in balancing work with family life. It is this richer understanding of the women's decision making and their experiences over this time period that is essential to developing policies to support these workers.

Notes

1. Johnson and Corcoran define a good job as one that is full time (at least 35 hours per week), pays at least $7 per hour (in 1999 dollars), and offers health benefits or is one that pays at least $8.50 per hour without benefits. If an individual's job satisfies either of these criteria except the number of hours, the job is "good" as long as the part-time employment is voluntary.

2. Most of these women, 76 percent, were employed at the wave 1 (Fall 1997) interview, while the other 24 percent were employed sometime in 1998. Of the group employed in 1998 ($n = 79$), we use the wage reported at the wave 2 interview in the majority of the cases (76 percent or $n = 60$), while the remaining 19 respondents were neither employed at the wave 1 or wave 2 interview but had been employed some time in between. Most of the individuals in the analysis sample, 85 percent, were employed at the wave 5 (Fall 2003) interview, but 50 respondents reported working in 2003 but had left or lost their jobs by the time of the wave 5 interview.

3. Another way to conceptualize low-wage work is to examine attributes of a job in addition to the wage rate. For example, jobs that pay relatively low wages are often thought of as being low skilled. Erickcek, Houseman, and Kalleberg (2002) define low-skilled jobs as those that "do not require postsecondary education and whose tasks can be learned on the job in a relatively short period of time." They do note that while low-skilled positions are not always low paid, a strong correlation does exist. Manufacturing jobs are often an exception. For many generations, high school graduates in a state like Michigan could find relatively high-paying jobs working on an automobile assembly line. The jobs required some amount of skill in operating the machinery, but for the most part, a new worker could go through a short training stint to learn how to do this.

4. Schochet and Rangarajan (2004) use data from the Survey of Income and Program Participation (SIPP) to look at pay growth experienced by a sample of individuals who started off working in low-wage jobs in 1996. They consider both males and females but not welfare recipients in particular.

5. For analysis purposes, all initial values are converted into 2003 dollars.

6. Schochet and Rangarajan (2004) use three different categories—low, medium, and high wages, with medium wages capturing those above the poverty line but less than 200 percent of the poverty line. However, the relatively small WES sample size makes it difficult to have so many cells in our analyses.

7. Based upon calculations using the "Marriage Calculator" available from the Administration for Children and Families of the U.S. Department of Health and Human Services.

8. Since the 2003 survey was conducted in the fall, it is possible that some of those who were surveyed, for example, in September or October got jobs in November or December and we did not observe this. However, to be categorized as unstably employed, a woman interviewed in September would have to have not worked at all between January and September 2003.

9. Indeed, women starting the study in above-poverty-wage jobs were more likely to have finished high school and to have additional schooling (about 41 percent of those starting in above-poverty-wage jobs as opposed to 31 percent of those beginning in lower-paying jobs). Women starting in above-poverty-wage jobs were also much more likely to never face transportation barriers (56 percent never lacked access to a car and always had a driver's license), while this was only true for 45 percent of those starting in lower-wage jobs. Significant differences also exist between these two groups on drug use and mental health problems, with women starting at poverty wages being 1) more likely to report drug use at baseline (whereas women starting in higher-paying jobs were more likely to report that they never used drugs during the study period) and 2) more likely to have persistent mental health problems.

10. As I note in Appendix A, regression coefficients represent a change in the natural log of the odds of being in one employment transition group relative to another. For simplicity's sake, I use the term odds as shorthand here.

11. The modal respondent was African American, between the ages of 25 and 34 in 1997, was never married, had two children in 1997 and never had more over the study period. She had some schooling beyond high school and had no human capital barriers. The modal respondent starting in a low-wage job never had any other employment barriers, while the modal respondent starting in a higher-wage job had a mental health problem in one or two waves.

12. Since being married was associated with a move from an above-poverty-wage job to unemployment, I tested to see if the race variable in this analysis might be picking up racial differences in marriage patterns. Recall that being African American was associated with an increased probability of remaining in a higher-wage job. African American women are less likely to marry than white women (Teachman, Tedrow, and Crowder 2000), and in the WES sample, racial differences in marriage are apparent: 28 percent of wave 5 white respondents were married by 2003 compared to 13.6 percent of African Americans. However, when I included a term interacting race and marriage, the coefficient was not significant (results not available).

4
Peeking inside the "Black Box" of Employment Transitions

At the start of the WES, many respondents could have conceivably been characterized as "long-term" welfare recipients. The average woman had spent more than half of her adult years with this support. Many had also experienced substantial portions of their childhood on welfare. By the end of 2003, nearly 80 percent of the sample had left welfare, although not all of those exits were permanent. Just under two-thirds of our sample experienced some level of wage growth, and many workers moved out of the "poverty wage" labor market (very narrowly defined). How did this happen?

The findings from the multivariate analyses presented in the previous chapter provide insights into some of the characteristics that are associated with various patterns of employment for former welfare recipients. However, the analyses of the survey data cannot tell us much about how women embarked on these pathways, the choices they made, and various obstacles and opportunities they might have encountered. This type of information is provided in the qualitative interviews, which allow us to peer more closely inside the "black box" of employment transitions. By better understanding women's decision making and their experiences over this time period, I argue, more effective policies to support low-wage workers can be developed.

This chapter describes the qualitative study sample, including the methods used for collecting and analyzing the data. Appendix B provides additional details about the methodology. I then introduce a number of the participants from the study, using their stories to trace out their employment paths. A number of the most relevant themes about work and family are highlighted and then expanded upon in the subsequent chapters.

THE WES QUALITATIVE SUPPLEMENT

In order to obtain more detailed information on the employment experiences of former welfare recipients, a qualitative component of WES was undertaken in early to mid-2004, after the final wave of survey data collection was completed. Thirty-two women, selected based on their employment histories and the ages of their children, were interviewed in depth about their experiences with work and raising children. More information about this sample follows. A greater explanation about selection into the qualitative sample and the methods used to code the data can be found in Appendix B.

Sample

Eighteen of the 32 women interviewed were African American, and the other 14 were white. Table 4.1 provides some basic demographic information on the sample, with comparisons to the larger WES sample. More detail is contained in Appendix B. As shown in Table B.1 in Appendix B, this distribution of 56.3 percent African American and 43.8 percent white is nearly the same as the racial breakdown of the larger survey sample, which is 56.4 percent African American and 45.4 percent white. Women ranged in age from 26 to 46, with a median age of 33. In 1997, when the study started, the vast majority, 75 percent, had at least one very young child living in the house; by 2003, only 15 percent of women in the qualitative sample had very young children, although most had one or two minor children living with them—one woman had seven children. Compared to the rest of the WES sample, qualitative sample members looked no different statistically in terms of the number and ages of their children.

Because I limited the qualitative sample to women with very steady employment records (see Appendix B), qualitative sample members, compared to the larger WES survey sample, worked in more months in each year of the survey; after 1997 qualitative respondents worked in almost every month, compared to about eight months for the rest of the sample (see Figure 4.1). As Figure 4.2 shows, the hourly wages of qualitative sample members track those of the rest of the sample, with the exception of the fifth and final survey wave in 2003. However, the

Table 4.1 Employment Barriers, Qualitative and Rest-of-WES Sample, as Measured in 1997

	Qualitative sample (%) (n = 32)	Rest of WES sample (%) (n = 504)
Human capital barrier		
Less than high school education	25.0	30.0
Learning disability	15.6	13.1
Low work experience	6.3	14.4
Work skills barrier	6.3	22.0*
Work norms barrier	9.4	8.5
Prior discrimination	12.5	14.9
Any human capital barrier	62.5	61.9
Mental health problem		
Major depression diagnosis	31.3	27.2
General anxiety disorder	3.2	7.8
Posttraumatic stress disorder	15.6	15.5
Drug dependence	3.1	4.4
Alcohol dependence	6.3	2.8
Any mental health problem	40.6	36.7
Physical health problem		
Mother's health problem	12.5	19.9
Child health problem	18.8	23.2
Any physical health problem	28.1	35.7
Work interference problem		
Domestic violence	12.5	16.3
Transportation problems	40.6	43.1
Drug use	37.5	21.0*
Other work interference problem	53.1	57.3

NOTE: * Difference significant at $p < 0.05$.
SOURCE: Author's tabulations from WES data.

range in hourly wage in 2003 was wide for the qualitative sample, from a low of about $3 for a woman receiving reimbursement from the state for providing day care for her sister's children to a high of around $19 for a couple of respondents. Hours worked by respondents also varied considerably. A few respondents reported working more than full time (e.g., 45–48 hours a week); 12 worked full time (40 hours a week);

Figure 4.1 Number of Months Worked per Year, WES Sample and Qualitative Sample

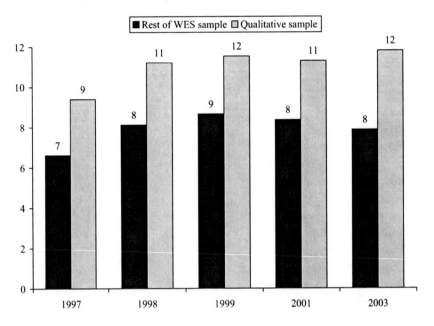

NOTE: Years represent the survey years.
SOURCE: Author's tabulations from WES data.

and 4 nearly full time (35–39 hours). However, 10 of the women in the qualitative sample worked under 35 hours a week.

Qualitative sample members worked in more months, and early analysis from the WES showed that the presence of various barriers was negatively related to employment (Danziger et al. 2000). Thus, I wondered if the qualitative sample was more "advantaged" in terms of the human capital members brought to the labor market as well as by their personal and family situations. Despite working more, qualitative sample members resembled the larger WES survey sample in terms of their education, skills, and physical and mental health challenges, although a few differences are present. On the one hand, qualitative sample members were very likely to have previously worked in jobs that met the Holzer definition of "skilled," as described in the previous chapter. On the other hand, a larger percentage of qualitative sample

**Figure 4.2 Median Hourly Wage Rates, WES Sample and
Qualitative Sample ($)**

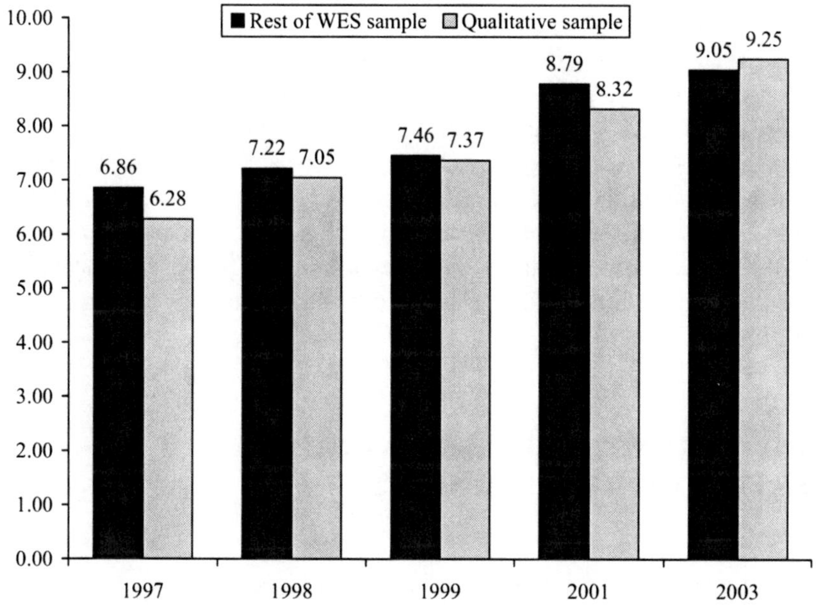

NOTE: Years represent the five survey years.
SOURCE: Author's tabulations from WES data.

members, 37.5 percent, reported using drugs, compared to about 21 percent of the rest of the sample.

In short, despite some restrictions placed on the construction of the qualitative sample (on a variety of demographic, human capital, health, and other measures), the women participating in the qualitative interviews looked remarkably similar to the WES sample. This does not mean that the findings from the qualitative sample are necessarily generalizable to the experiences of all WES sample members or to former welfare recipients more broadly. However, I show these similarities to demonstrate that the qualitative supplement did not necessarily comprise the "best" cases or the most "successful" cases in terms of outcomes post–welfare reform. Rather, they represent a variety of employment experiences.

Data Collection

The interviews for the qualitative supplement, like the WES surveys, generally took place in women's homes and lasted about 90 minutes. The questions covered a range of topics, including impressions of what constituted a good and a bad job, what women liked and disliked most about their jobs, how well (or not) they got along with supervisors and co-workers, how they made decisions about their employment, and what aspirations they held for their futures. Through this qualitative inquiry, I hope to be able to provide, as Angel, Lein, and Henrici (2006) note, "deeper insights" into the factors that give rise to particular employment patterns and "the subjective reality that lies behind them" (p. 15).

WHAT CAN WE LEARN FROM WOMEN'S EMPLOYMENT EXPERIENCES?

The women we interviewed in depth represented a wide array of employment experiences. Seven were employed in food services, four of those specifically in fast-food chains. Four had housekeeping jobs, either in hotels, hospitals, or in private homes. Another four worked in health services, in jobs ranging from health care aides to a licensed practical nurse (LPN). Three worked for transportation companies in management, dispatching, and assistance roles, and another three were cashiers in retail outlets. Two worked in manufacturing jobs, two in public safety/security, and six in other occupations, ranging from a day care provider to a pharmacy technician. Finally, one of the women, although working when surveyed in the fall of 2003, was unemployed when the qualitative interviews were conducted in spring 2004.

As in the analyses presented earlier (see Tables 3.2 and 3.3), I divided the women in the qualitative study into five groups: those who progressed from a low-wage job into a higher-paying one, those who stayed in a low-wage job, those who moved from a higher-paying job to a lower one, those who did well in both periods, and those who lost jobs by the end (see Table 4.2). All of the names used in this and other chapters are pseudonyms. In addition, certain details about jobs and families

Table 4.2 Employment Transitions, 1997/98 to 2003, for Qualitative Sample Members (*n* = 32)

Transition type	Number
Poverty wage both periods	10
Poverty wage to above-poverty wage	11
Poverty wage to unemployment	1
Above-poverty wage both periods	6
Above-poverty wage to poverty wage	4
Above-poverty wage to unemployment	0

NOTE: A poverty-wage job is equivalent to $6.15 an hour or less in 1997 and $7.05 an hour in 2003.
SOURCE: Author's tabulations from WES data.

have been changed to protect individuals' identities. In these stories, I also note the various barriers that the surveys identified these women as having and the ways in which women did (or, as was often the case, did not) recognize the challenges as having an impact on employment.

Poverty Wage to Above-Poverty Wage

Lorraine is an example of one of the 11 women in the qualitative sample who moved from a lower-paying job to a higher-paying one. Lorraine never finished high school, dropping out when she became pregnant at 16 and going on welfare. When the study started, she worked at a series of cashier jobs, making just over the minimum wage at all of them. In 1999 she was alerted by her sister about an opening for a janitorial position within a large local hospital where her sister worked. The position paid more than $7 an hour, at the low end of our cutoff for an "above-poverty-wage" job, but nevertheless an improvement over her previous wages. She received two raises, and by the end of our study was making about $8.50 an hour. However, the higher wages were not why she reported taking the job. At first she told us that she looked upon the hospital position as an opportunity to learn new skills, to try her hand at something she had never done before. However, more questioning led to the real reason: as a cashier, Lorraine often worked the second shift, leaving her children on their own after school. The unsupervised time, she believed, resulted in poor academic performances, and Lorraine decided that she should find a job that allowed her to monitor her children's homework and be with them when they returned home from school.

Although Lorraine thought that her lack of education prevented her from obtaining an even higher-paying job, none of the other challenges documented by the survey were a part of her narrative. Lorraine was one of the women who, at least initially, did not know many workplace norms. She also met the criteria for having mental health and transportation problems at one or two of the survey waves. Rather, it was concern about her children's school performance that prompted her to look for a different job.

Regina, too, started in a lower-wage job and worked up the employment ladder. Instead of attributing her climb to any of her own characteristics, she claimed that she got her job through connections. She reported that she was employed as a facilities manager of a convention center because she was romantically involved with the person doing the hiring. This change took her from a less-than-minimum wage, off-the-books job as a maid into a situation in which she became a supervisor, obtained health benefits, and saw her wage rise to more than $10 an hour. While Regina noted that the higher pay was important in her decision to switch jobs, also of priority was the work schedule, which was first shift.

Additionally, although she said that her current employment at the convention center was stressful, in that many of her tasks had to be completed on short notice or in a small amount of time, Regina believed it was much less of a strain than some of her previous jobs, including a stint working on the night shift at a convenience store. On that job, she was held up at gunpoint. She quit immediately thereafter. While Regina had mental health problems at a couple of times during the WES data collection, I was not able to ascertain whether or not the robbery at her previous job and her reports of stress at work were related.

Tia spent the early years of the WES moving from one low-wage job to another. She characterized her early employment trajectory as "Just working all these deadbeat jobs that weren't paying anything for all these hours."[1] At the time she was making these lateral moves, however, Tia returned to school to complete a certificate program in health care, a credential that, interestingly, is not captured by the survey. When we interviewed her, she was working as a medical secretary, making more than $15 an hour. Nevertheless, Tia believed that she would not have been able to handle work, family, and school responsibilities without significant help from the father of her children (and now her husband). She described him as an active participant in the children's lives, assisting them with homework so that she could complete her own: "You couldn't ask for a better dad, as far as homework that's not done—he takes [the kids] and he's going to put them on that computer and he'll say, 'We're doing this, this, this.' As far as projects, he'll get down to the basement so I can be upstairs finishing my work."

Lorraine, Regina, and Tia eventually found higher-paying jobs by moving from one employer to another, with few breaks in their work history. Some of the literature suggests that moving from one job to another may be the best strategy for mobility out of the low-wage labor market (Andersson, Holzer, and Lane 2005; Loprest 1992; Neal 1999; Topel and Ward 1992). In part this may be related to changes in the employment market. Recent research has documented increased "stickiness" among lower-skilled service-sector jobs. That is, opportunities for advancement within a particular firm are limited, and on-the-job training, which might provide skills to move up within the organization (or to a different employer), is minimal (Bernhardt et al. 2001).

However, I found many women who were able to advance by staying at the same job and getting raises or by being promoted. Barbara started working for a trucking company in 1998 in a clerical position. She made less than $6 an hour, although she worked a great deal of overtime. By 2001, she was a manager earning $14 an hour with benefits. Jackie had worked in the same grocery store for about five years, but several years ago she was promoted into an assistant manager position. A raise that accompanied the promotion, coupled with yearly wage increases that kept pace with the cost of living, resulted in a change in the categorization of her job from poverty-wage to above-poverty-wage. Jackie believed she could have made even more money as a supervisor, but doing so would have entailed a commute to a more distant store, something she did not want to do, largely because of her daughter. Physical and mental health problems, which the survey found, were again not part of the story she told about her work decisions.

Continuous Poverty-Wage Employment

A nearly equal number of women in the qualitative sample remained working in very low-wage jobs as progressed to higher-paying positions. Some of these individuals had been in the same position
for four years or longer, while others moved from job to job, trying to
improve their lot. Two were getting paid by the state to take care of disabled relatives. Mishon made just above the minimum wage when she
started working as a hotel housekeeper in 1997. Although she quit for a
period of a year, she went back to the hotel in 2000 and was still working there when we interviewed her. When asked if anything in her job
had changed in the past year, Mishon replied that no, "Everything is the
same." What was also the same was her pay, which had increased only
by about 50¢ per hour over the years. However, she had been given a
new title of assistant manager, prompting her to tell us that yes, she had
advanced on the employment ladder.

Looking at how women fared by comparing their wages in 1997 to
those in 2003 sometimes masks the bumpy road that they faced along
the way. Anita had a job as a machine operator in an auto supply plant,
and by 1999 she was making more than $8 an hour. However, she be-
came frustrated at the slow rate at which her pay was rising, saying,
"I was there, like, five years, and we was just getting 17¢ raises, 12¢
raises. We were in a factory, we were doing car parts and stuff. I'm like,
it's not worth it. I had enough there!" Unfortunately, as a high school
dropout, the jobs she could find subsequently were even lower paying.
When we met with her in early 2004 she was working part time at a fast
food establishment. While she had married, her husband's wages were
also relatively low, and child support obligations to his other children
meant that their finances were always tight.

Maylene, a self-professed "honest worker," had bounced around
from job to job, often, it turned out, due to conflicts with her employers
over schedules or perceived unfairness. As she told her interviewer Amber, on her last job in a factory she worked "sunup to sundown, Sunday
through Sunday." Frustrated by her inability to get time off (overtime
was seemingly required) to tend to errands and to her family, Maylene
quit. Maylene also left positions because employers asked her to do
work she believed to be outside her job description or because she got
"bad vibes" from co-workers. Indeed, Maylene might have exempli-

fied the type of welfare recipient that many policymakers worried about in the years after implementation of welfare reform: the person who could get jobs but not keep them because of interpersonal difficulties. However, Maylene stressed repeatedly that her foremost responsibility was to her family, noting that jobs were easy to come by but she only had one family. When we spoke with her in 2004, she was getting paid about $130 a week by the state to care for her bedridden grandmother. However, like Sierra, the other woman in our sample who was taking care of a disabled relative, Maylene had a few sidelines. Maylene supplemented her income by providing day care; Sierra hustled for various odd jobs, or "little things I've got going," when she had a bill that needed paying and money was tight.

The WES survey data document that both Anita and Maylene had multiple challenges. In addition to their lack of education, both had mental health problems the majority of the time, both had periodic transportation difficulties, and both were frequent drug users. It is easy to imagine that any of these problems could account for their frustrations. For example, Maylene's conflicts with her employers might have been exacerbated by her depression. However, her rationale that family came first was a sentiment shared by many other women in the study, regardless of the types of employment barriers the survey may have found.

Above-Poverty Wage to Poverty Wage

For other women in our qualitative sample, the movement on the employment ladder was downward. As noted earlier, more than a third of WES workers saw their wages decrease, and many who started in above-poverty-wage work ended up in poverty-wage jobs by the time we concluded the study. Four women in the qualitative sample experienced this downward transition. Janelle was one of these individuals. In 1997, Janelle left welfare for a job in an auto manufacturing plant. The commute was very lengthy, upward of two hours each way, so she quit and returned to welfare, receiving benefits on and off through 2000. Although she was working most of this time, her wages were around $6 an hour, low enough to qualify her and her four children for Temporary Assistance to Needy Families (TANF). A friend alerted her about a job opening as a maid in a local hotel. The pay, about $7 an hour, was not anywhere near the $17 she was making at the plant. However, the location was very close to her home, and she found the work easy. While Janelle did not lack transportation—the survey found that she had no barriers to employment—the length of time she needed to be in the car to get to a higher-paying job was not worth the effort to her.

Not all downward moves were necessarily detrimental. Kathleen quit a relatively well-paid job ($9.50 an hour) as a receptionist in an office, in large part because she did not get along with her co-workers. When interviewed, she was working in a day care center. Although her pay was only slightly above minimum wage, Kathleen loved working with children and was able to place her son in care at the center, free of charge. She called it her "dream job." However, the fact that her husband had a very high-paying job, and no obligations to children from other relationships, likely enabled her to take a job she loved rather than one that paid better. Most women we interviewed were not in Kathleen's situation.

A few women experienced downward employment mobility even though they remained in the same job. Denise, a caregiver in a group home, had worked for the same company for quite a few years but had not received much in the way of additional pay. Purported financial difficulties led Denise's employers to lower her hourly wage from nearly $8 to $6.50. When we interviewed her, Denise repeatedly used the word "frustrated" to describe how she felt about her job. However, she never mentioned the pay cut as the reason for her dissatisfaction. Rather, she talked extensively about feeling marginalized by her co-workers, whom she described as "cliquish," and snubbed by her supervisors, who she believed gave prime shifts to their favorite employees. While Denise never reported that she felt any workplace discrimination (as measured in the survey), she believed that the actions of her co-workers and bosses were preventing her from advancing.

Similarly, Ellen firmly believed that favoritism at her place of work, a clothing store, kept her from getting promotions and a better schedule. Over the course of the study, Ellen's wage stayed roughly the same, hovering around $6 an hour; with inflation, this amounted to a decrease in pay over the years. She had worked in a variety of jobs initially but had been with the same employer for about three years when we interviewed her. Ellen was one of the few individuals in the qualitative sample who had "low work experience," which is among the key variables in the multivariate analyses that distinguished women who advanced and those who did not. By working steadily between 1997 and 2003, she certainly accumulated a great deal of employment experience and never identified this as a challenge to further advancement.

Continuous Above-Poverty-Wage Employment

Six of the women interviewed worked in above-poverty-wage jobs throughout the 1997–2004 period in which we observed them. Recall again that "above-poverty wage" is simply defined as more than $7.05 an hour in 2003.

Two of these women worked for auto-parts manufacturers, the quintessential "good" job in Michigan for people without postsecondary schooling. Johnetta made nearly $12 an hour and had just had her six-year anniversary at the plant when we interviewed her (although she was briefly laid off for a time in 1998). Interestingly, Johnetta never mentioned the pay as the reason for applying for the job. Instead she said she thought that "it would be a good job for a single mother." Initially, Johnetta's shifts were four 10-hour days, leaving her free on Fridays to schedule doctors' appointments for her son. Although her son had physical health problems throughout the study, Johnetta's arrangement allowed her to accommodate his health needs while not missing work.

However, even some of the women in higher-paying jobs worried about their prospects for the future. Toni, who worked as an aide in a local elementary school, had been a long-term welfare recipient when she noticed that the rules were beginning to change. She told me that, in the mid-1990s, when she heard that the welfare agency would soon no longer allow participation in education and training to fulfill the work requirement, she quickly completed her GED. Once welfare required women to work, she said, "My caseworker didn't need to tell me to get a job." With the exception of a short time in 1998 when she was employed in fast food and earned just over the minimum wage, Toni's jobs had paid fairly well. When I interviewed her in 2004, she was making more than $11 an hour. However, the school board had been laying off support personnel, and Toni thought she might lose her position. She knew that with only a GED, her prospects for a job paying equally well were slim. As did many other women we interviewed, she talked vaguely of going back to school but did not have an idea of where and what field she might study. In the meantime, again like so many women in this study, making sure her teenaged sons did well in school and stayed out of trouble was Toni's primary concern.

Unemployment

We selected our subjects from a pool of women who had jobs at the time the final survey was administered in the fall of 2003. However, several months later when we went to interview her, one of the individuals in our qualitative sample had lost her job, putting her in the category of transitions into unstable employment. Brenda, in her early thirties, had seen her wages rise over the years as she worked as a health care aide, first for one employer and then another. A series of health problems of her own and of several family members led her to quit her job so that she could take care of herself, her mother, and her daughter. For Brenda, it was easier to quit her job and try to find a new one than to attempt to negotiate time off with her employer. Also, for Brenda, responsibilities to her family came first, a message we heard repeatedly in these interviews.

This brief overview of some of the women's stories represents the major themes we uncovered in our interviews. Although satisfactory pay is certainly an important component of a "good" job, women considered many other aspects—schedules, commute times, workplace environment—when making decisions about whether to take a new position or stay in their current one. The next chapter explores in greater depth these other characteristics of jobs, as well as provides more detailed descriptions of what women actually do in their work and how their own employment experiences might influence decisions about career advancement. As some of the women's narratives demonstrate, work schedules, particularly as they relate to children's needs, are one of the more important factors that individuals in our sample considered, regardless of the number or ages of those children. Many women knew that their lack of education held them back; some were trying to figure out if they could manage work, school, and family. Interestingly, with the exception of education, very few women talked about other "employment barriers" as potentially affecting their prospects. Even though I focused on these characteristics in the previous chapter as a way to parse out potential factors that might be associated with different career trajectories (and also used them to describe this sample), domestic violence, mental health problems, and drug use were rarely discussed, and if they were, the context was not about employment. Rather, it is the shared experiences of struggling to maintain dignity and to be a good mother while working in the low-wage and low-skilled labor market that emerged as most salient.

Note

1. All quotes are verbatim responses of the respondents, as transcribed.

5
What Working Mothers Want

Attributes of Good Jobs

In the context of employment advancement, the previous chapters, as well as much of the prior research in this area, have focused primarily on wages as the key attribute of a "good" job. Indeed, nearly all of the women we interviewed in depth said that they would sort jobs into "good" or "bad" by their pay. However, remuneration was only one dimension women considered in assessing job quality. In this chapter, I analyze data from the qualitative interviews related to the question, what makes a job good?

WHAT MAKES A JOB GOOD?

All of the women interviewed agreed that the pay rate was an important factor in determining the quality of a job. Although the women's benchmark for good pay varied, by and large it was modest. Most agreed that a good job pays enough to survive, and at least $10 an hour was the generally agreed-upon wage at which women thought they could exist comfortably while supporting a family. As Amanda, a legal office worker, explained, "Oh, I'm thinking minimum start off would be $10 an hour to even just survive, which you don't really at that price. If I was a single woman, shoot! Ten bucks an hour would be sweet." Other women defined as good "a job where you're not struggling day to day." Still others believed good earnings meant having money left over after paying the bills. Olivia, a mother of three children, explained, "I think for me [good pay is] enough to pay your bills and then still take a vacation."

Similarly, benefits, particularly health insurance, were also important attributes of jobs. Some women indicated a willingness to earn a lower hourly wage if they would be able to procure health insurance.

The type of health insurance desired was also seemingly quite reasonable. Melanie, who worked in the transportation business, told us that she didn't need dental insurance or vision care because, "That's something you're always seeing coupons [for], and you can kind of just put up and save to the side for those." Medical insurance, though, she said, is something "you will always need."

Despite these rather limited requirements related to pay and benefits, few women in the qualitative sample, and in the larger WES, were paid more than $10 an hour, and a majority did not have employer-provided health insurance. Among the 32 women we interviewed in depth, just 13 had achieved an hourly wage rate of at least $10 by 2003, despite the fact that most had been more or less steadily employed since 1997. Less than half, 15 women total, were working in jobs *offering* health insurance. Among those whose employers offered insurance, only 9 took the coverage. Others, like LaVonda, who worked in fast food, believed they could not afford their employers' plans. As she noted, "They [the employer] offer something, but it's—I don't know, it was, like, over $50 a week or something like that . . . it was a lot [of money]. And I just kind of laughed at it and I didn't even finish reading the stuff on it. I was like, there ain't no way I can afford that." A few other women were unable to access their employers' health benefits because they fell short of working the minimum number of hours required to be eligible. Toni, who worked for a local school district, reported that she would need to work at least six hours a day to qualify for benefits. Her job as a teacher's aide, though, was only scheduled for five hours a day. Slightly more women in the qualitative sample, 16, were receiving Medicaid, and even those who took private coverage often had children receiving health insurance through Medicaid. Seven women went without health insurance.

The growth in the number of uninsured Americans has received widespread attention in the media and is a source of concern for policymakers. As health care costs have risen, many employers have ceased to offer private coverage to their employees, or, as was the case for LaVonda, charge premiums that may be out of reach for low-wage employees. Prior to welfare reform, recipients were basically assured health care coverage through Medicaid, as Aid to Families with Dependent Children (AFDC) recipients were categorically eligible for the program. The Personal Responsibility and Work Opportunity Reconciliation Act (PRWORA) "delinked" Medicaid from the new welfare program, Temporary Assistance to Needy Families (TANF). In part, this was done so that poor children would not be without health care coverage if their parents lost welfare benefits due to sanctions or time limits (Mann 1999). However, some advocates worried that the delinking would result in underutilization of the program, particularly for those families who perceived dealing with the welfare system as being too much of a hassle.[1] For those who are willing to use public benefits, though, Medicaid may only cover children in the family. Although Medicaid does cover low-income adults with children, income eligibility thresholds are quite low. According to the Center on Budget and Policy Priorities, in the median state, a parent is eligible for Medicaid only if her income is less than 69 percent of the poverty line (Ku 2005). Children, on the other hand, are much more likely to be covered, either through the Medicaid program or through the State Child Health Insurance Program (SCHIP). Most states now cover children living in households with income up to 200 percent of the poverty line. In the WES, we find health care coverage rates for children at more than 96 percent.

While less often discussed, some women desired additional features, including paid vacation days, sick days, and retirement benefits. A number of women were already starting to worry about their retirement. Caroline was 38 years old when we talked to her in the spring of 2004. She had been working full time as a registered nurse for nearly four years and was the highest-paid worker we interviewed. Although her pay and full-time employment status left her much better off financially than many other women in the study, she still had concerns for her future and wished her employer offered her a retirement package. As she stated, "I used to focus more on the pay, but as I'm getting older I'm finding that benefits, good benefits, are really crucial. You need retirement funds, and I'm starting to realize [that] now. When I was younger, you know, you don't foresee the future, you don't even think about that. But now I'm finding that as I'm getting older, I need something to fall back on. So that is becoming, like, number one on my list. Where am I going to find employment where I can work and come out with a good retirement fund and insurance benefits?"

Johnetta was employed on the line for one of Michigan's Big Three car companies. Alongside her worked a 60-year-old woman, whom Johnetta described as unable to retire because she was still living from paycheck to paycheck. This woman's situation frightened Johnetta, who said, "You know, I'm getting older, too . . . and I'm looking at her thinking, I don't want to be that age struggling like that. You know, so it's like a learning experience for me to be around older women that are out there stuck. I don't want to be stuck." Unfortunately for Johnetta, persistent declines in the state's automotive industry led several of the companies, including General Motors and Ford, to continue to close plants and otherwise downsize their workforces. Furthermore, Johnetta was not a union member and did not receive health or any other benefits, potentially increasing the likelihood that she could find herself "stuck" as well.

Aside from pay and benefits, though, many women evaluated employment on other, less tangible factors. Another very commonly cited characteristic of a good job was having positive relationships with co-workers and supervisors. Women described co-workers at a hypothetical good job as understanding, reliable, nice, friendly, easy to talk to, respectful, and team players. The general consensus was that working with positive people who are easy to get along with makes a job more enjoyable. Shanice, another woman who was employed in the local school system, told us why good co-workers were so important. She said, "I would like a job where I would be able to get along with everybody because less tension makes a more productive work space, and when I don't have to deal with tension and everybody gets along, I think it's better to work there. You enjoy going to work instead of dreading going to work everyday because you have to deal with certain people."

A possible explanation for this finding—that women cited a pleasant work environment as an important contributor to a good job—is that most women we spoke to had at least one story about past and ongoing serious problems with customers, co-workers, and/or supervisors. In some ways, this is not all that surprising. Anyone who has been in the workforce for a certain length of time is likely to have encountered a boss who could not be pleased or co-workers who seemed to go out of their way to make the workplace miserable. Since many women were currently working or had recent experience in service-sector jobs, we might also expect to hear numerous stories about rude or demanding customers. However, the tenor of some of the narratives about workplace strife was quite grim. Women described situations where favoritism and unfairness, for example, around scheduling and task assignment, were rampant, severe verbal abuse was not uncommon, and harassment and discrimination were part of the job.

"MY BOSS, SHE HAS THESE MOOD SWINGS"

Wendy was a 40-year-old divorced mother of two teenaged sons and one adult daughter. She spent a good deal of her early adult years on and off welfare, although she held a series of jobs in a variety of local restaurants and bars. When we interviewed her in 2004, she was employed full time as a bartender in a family-owned establishment. Although Wendy was earning more money than she had in all of the years the WES had followed her, the stress and strain of the place was starting to wear on her. Wendy suspected that many of the restaurant's policies were actually illegal. For example, she told us that no one was allowed a break, nor was anyone allowed to sit down during a shift. During downtimes, wait-staff were supposed to wash the walls, clean the windows, and refill the condiments. In her 23 years in the serving business, Wendy had never experienced such treatment. Furthermore, she reported that the owners discouraged fraternization among the staff. She said, "They don't want you congregating and talking. They don't want the waitresses being friends with each other."

Perhaps most challenging for Wendy was dealing with the owner's girlfriend, whom Wendy described as mean-tempered and verbally abusive, particularly when she had been drinking. Wendy noted that busy nights were particularly difficult: "When it's really busy, she [the owner's girlfriend] freaks out. If she has to hostess, she'll run from one end of the restaurant to the bar and get a Bud Light and a shot of Jack Daniels—she drinks all night. So the drunker she gets, the ornerier she gets. And then she tries to snap at you." Another night, the boyfriend of Wendy's pregnant daughter called the restaurant, looking for Wendy because her daughter was about to undergo an emergency cesarean section. The owner's girlfriend answered the phone, and, according to Wendy's account, told him that Wendy was busy and hung up. Wendy did not find out until three hours later that she was a grandmother. She recounted her reaction by noting, "My first thought was to punch her in the face and leave, but I controlled my temper over the years. As I

walked back there, I thought, she's got way more money than I do. If I
do anything to her, I'm going to be put in jail and I won't see the baby,
so I better be nice and not do anything to her!"

I use Wendy's story as an illustration of some of the difficulties
many of the women we interviewed faced while at work. Reports of
hostile bosses were not uncommon among the qualitative sample. A
quick survey of the language used to describe such colleagues includes
"Dr. Jekyll and Mr. Hyde," "paranoid," "a bully," "ornery" (used by
three different women to describe their respective supervisors), and "a
liar." One might ask why Wendy and other women put up with this kind
of aggravation at work. For Wendy, it may have been because she lived
in a more rural area, with relatively few employment options. Wendy
also told us that the pay was good and in general the manager worked
with her to set up a schedule that met her needs (a subject I turn to later
in the chapter). However, Wendy, along with many of the other women
we interviewed, might have believed that incidents like this were just
part of what one has to tolerate in the low-wage labor market, particularly when jobs become more scarce. A number of women told us that
they felt lucky to be employed, even if their current jobs are not ideal.
While a few individuals reported that they at times fought back, most
either chose to ignore their bosses as best as they could or found other
ways to cope. As LaVonda, a fast-food worker, noted when talking about
her verbally abusive supervisor, "Well, I pretty much have to keep my
mouth shut. I need my job . . . so I just grit my teeth and grin and bear
it, but she can be a little too much sometimes, in my opinion."

Johnetta and Shanice, introduced earlier in this chapter, as well as
Ellen, a 40-year-old white woman, all believed that they had experienced racial discrimination on their jobs, some of it subtle, some out-
right. Johnetta was one of only a small number of African Americans
working in the plant, despite the high proportion of African Americans
in the larger community. She believed that when layoffs occurred, African Americans were more likely to be let go and once called in the
local unit of the National Association for the Advancement of Colored
People (NAACP) to investigate. However, nothing came of this, and
Johnetta said that she had resolved to "change my mind-set" and be
"grateful, thankful" that she still had a job. Shanice, also African American, had filed a grievance against her supervisor, who had used a racial
slur in front of her. Nothing, to Shanice's knowledge, ever resulted from

this either. Shanice tried to limit her involvement with her supervisor, although it was very clear in talking to her that she remained upset by that person's failure to ever apologize. Ellen, a white woman, had been employed at a retail clothing store for about two years and also perceived discrimination in her workplace. She reported that all of her co-workers, except the other white employee, were invited to holiday parties held by her supervisor, and that the supervisor saved the "best" shifts for other African Americans. Ellen claimed to have overheard her supervisor say that she was "going to make sure she takes care of her own first."

That discrimination and harassment in the workplace occurs, particularly directed against racial/ethnic minorities and women, should not be surprising. A study conducted in the late 1980s finds that many employers harbored negative views about the skill levels of inner-city and African American job applicants (Neckerman and Kirschenman 1991). Once on the job, African Americans face an increased risk for racial discrimination. A survey of Los Angeles residents finds that almost half of African Americans reported that they worked under supervisors who used racial slurs, perceived themselves to have gotten raises or promotions at a slower pace compared to other racial groups, and/or had experienced general racial discrimination (Bobo and Suh 2000).

We adapted the questions from the Los Angeles survey for the WES. At each survey wave we asked whether our respondents believed that they had not been hired, been fired, or not been promoted because of their race, sex, or welfare status. They were also asked if on their current or most recent job their supervisor made racial slurs, insulting remarks about women or about welfare recipients (in later waves we also asked if co-workers or customers engaged in this behavior). We asked global questions about whether they believed they had experienced racial or gender discrimination on their jobs or had been discriminated against because of their current or recent welfare status. We also asked whether they had been sexually harassed at work.

Looking across all waves, and as shown in Table 5.1, we find that just under a third, 31.4 percent, of the entire survey sample ($n = 536$) reported that at least some time during the study, their supervisors, co-workers, and/or customers used racial slurs or made derogatory comments about women. Slightly less, 29.5 percent, reported that they had faced discrimination on the job because of their gender, with

Table 5.1 **Experiences of Prior Discrimination among WES**
Respondents, as Measured in 1997–2003 (n = 536)

	WES sample (%)	Qualitative sample (%)
Supervisor/co-worker used racial slurs and/or made derogatory comments about women	31.4	56.3
Experience of gender discrimination	29.5	50.0
Experience of racial discrimination	13.4	21.9
African American respondents	18.5	—
White respondents	7.6	—
Sexual harassment	11.6	28.1

SOURCE: Author's tabulations from WES data.

white women being slightly more likely to report this. Reports of racial discrimination in the workplace were more rare: 13.4 percent of the sample respondents at some point during the study believed that they had either not been offered a job or had been turned down for a promotion or pay raise or otherwise treated unfairly because of their race. Not surprisingly, African American women were much more likely to report such experiences, with 18.5 percent of all African Americans saying they had faced this type of treatment. However, a few white women (7.6 percent), like Ellen, also reported racial discrimination. The proportion of women reporting that they had been sexually harassed while working was even lower, 11.6 percent.

If we look at these same data for just the women participating in the qualitative study, we find much higher reports on some of the items. For example, half of all the women we interviewed in depth reported gender discrimination, and more than half reported that they worked in places where supervisors or co-workers used slurs. Proportionately more reported harassment (28 percent), and more reported discrimination (22 percent). Of course, some of the difference is just due to the small sample size of the qualitative study. Alternatively, because the women in the qualitative sample have worked more than the sample as a whole, it could be that they have simply had more exposure to situations where they could experience discrimination. Another possibility is that the women we interviewed in depth may be different from the rest of the sample on this dimension, which might mean that the reader should interpret this set of findings about difficulties in the workplace with some amount of caution. However, the survey questions on discrimination and harassment were very pointed and specific, including questions such as the following: 1) "On your main job, were you ever sexually harassed?" 2) "On this job, have you ever been discriminated against because of your race or ethnic origin?" 3) "Have others at your place of employment [received] promotions or pay raises faster than you because of their race or ethnic origin?" These types of questions were unlikely to pick up the day-to-day pettiness and difficulties described by so many women we interviewed.

Not surprisingly then, the majority of the 32 women we interviewed told us that they believed their jobs to be stressful, and for some, co-workers and supervisors were the direct cause of that strain. Tia, for example, held a midlevel clerical position in a large area hospital. By the time we interviewed her, she had moved up considerably from a minimum-wage reception job in another company to her current position, where she was making more than $15 an hour. Yet her relatively high wage did not protect her from this type of workplace strife. For more than a year, Tia's counterpart on another shift would tell their boss that Tia was not getting her work done during her shift. Tia and other co-workers speculated that this woman, a 30-year veteran of the hospital, might have felt threatened by her. However, what made Tia feel worse—worse than being "set up" by her colleague—was that her supervisor sided with the co-worker. It took her supervisor a year before she finally looked more closely into the situation and found that Tia was, indeed, doing all of her work.

Given all of these experiences, it is not surprising that, when asked to define the qualities that make a job "good," more than half of all of the women we interviewed in depth said that a good job is one with a positive working environment, where co-workers enjoy one another, and, in the words of Amanda, others "respect you and treat you decently." Yet, we found that these considerations were not consistent norms of operation on the jobs held by many of the women. On the other hand, the individuals' experiences, even in the most stressful work environments, were not uniformly negative. In the next section, I describe some of the benefits women derived from their jobs. While I do not want to glamorize the low-wage labor market, it is important to understand the meaning that work can and does provide for at least some of the women we interviewed.

WHY WORK IN A LOW-WAGE JOB? THE MEANING OF HELPING

The aging of America and the growth of the service sector more generally have provided job opportunities for many former welfare recipients. Advances in medical technology have contributed to increased life expectancy in the United States. According to data from the National Center for Health Statistics, the average 65-year-old in 1960 was only projected to live another 14 years, to age 79, and many people did not make it to age 65, since life expectancy at birth for that cohort was about 50 years (Arias 2007). Today's 65-year-olds can be expected to live another 19 years, to age 84, and many more adults are living to 65. As our country ages, demand for health care services has grown, including those provided by assisted living facilities, nursing homes, and companies offering home health care. The Bureau of Labor Statistics (2007) predicts that employment in the health care industry will grow at a rate of 28 percent in the 10-year period between 2006 and 2016. Within this sector, the occupation with the largest projected growth is home health aides, who tend to be the lowest paid.

Similar trends are more difficult to assemble for workers who are employed in jobs such as cashiering in retail or fast-food establishments, since these jobs cross industry and occupational codes. Service jobs encompass a wide range of activities, from banking to window washing, and pay a broad range of wages (Thurow and Waldstein 1989). However, it is commonly acknowledged that employment for less-educated workers in the United States has shifted away from manufacturing and toward service sector work.

Perhaps no one job typifies service sector employment more than fast-food workers. Indeed, the terms "burger flipper" or "McJob," a not-so-subtle reference to McDonald's, are often used as shorthand for many types of low-wage jobs, with the implication that, at most, the only skill needed for such positions is the ability to hold a spatula and turn a hamburger. Much of the language used to describe low-wage jobs and the tasks associated with them conveys a sense that the work is demeaning: low-wage workers often perform tasks that are repetitive, leave little room in which to exercise judgment, and, in some cases, are jobs that no one else wants to do. Journalist Barbara Ehrenreich spent a year working "undercover" in a series of low-wage jobs, including as a house cleaner for a cleaning service and as a nurse's aide at a home for the elderly (Ehrenreich 2001). As a maid, Ehrenreich was told exactly how to vacuum (in a fanlike pattern), how much water to use when cleaning floors (not very much), and was subject to having her behavior closely monitored (some home owners placed video cameras in their residences and reported back to the company on the conduct of the maids.) As a nurse's aide, Ehrenreich was faced with performing backbreaking and often dirty tasks, such as cleaning bedpans and the backsides of the residents. Breaks, if given, were short in duration, while rules were plentiful. It is no wonder that Ehrenreich, like many others, refers to people who work permanently in these jobs as "wage slaves."

Denise, a 32-year-old African American mother of three, has worked since 2000 as an aide in a residential facility for mentally handicapped adults. Like many other women, including Ehrenreich, she found her workplace to be less than ideal. It was a family-run operation, which Denise said meant that only family members got the prime shifts as well as management positions and higher pay. Denise told us that one reason she stayed in this situation was that she had "quit too many jobs" and was determined to have some stability in her employment record. Becoming a mother at age 15 derailed Denise's plans to be a nurse. As an aide, Denise was responsible for bathing, clothing, and preparing meals for and feeding the residents, many of whom were on special diets or had other illnesses. She also had to clean, including doing laundry and tidying the kitchen. Although Denise's medical training was limited to basic first aid and cardiopulmonary resuscitation (CPR) and she lacked a high school diploma, she was also responsible for dispensing medication and changing and cleaning colonoscopy bags of several of the residents. For this, she made a little under $7 an hour.

As we talked more with Denise, it became clear that a strong motivating factor behind her decision to remain at this job was the interactions with the facility's residents and her ability to assist them. When asked what she liked best about her work, she unequivocally answered that it allowed her to help others, in this case, a group of people with some very severe limitations. She spoke of one resident who looked forward to Denise being on duty, because Denise took extra time to "wash her hair right." Another resident greeted Denise by throwing her arms around her and saying "I love you!" Other than her ability to help others, Denise said, "I really don't like my job."

About a third of the women we interviewed were employed in jobs that could be considered "helping" positions. These included nurses and nurse's aides like Denise, women who worked in schools, as well as those who were day care providers. For many of these women, being able to assist others provided meaning to their employment experiences. Melanie made about $10 an hour as a transportation dispatcher for a private ride service that took the elderly and the disabled to doctors' appointments and on various errands. While Melanie's job was to answer calls from people wishing to arrange rides and to set up schedules for the drivers, she took it upon herself to go the extra mile to get to know her customers. Many of the service's users, particularly the elderly, were very lonely, and Melanie knew that she might be the only person they talked to that day. When possible, she took a little extra time to chat with her regular customers, getting to know them better, and checking up on them. Periodically, she reported that she would go out to the vans or tag along on a route so that she could meet her customers in person. Her efforts were appreciated; she told us that she received thank-you cards from the seniors, some sent directly to her boss so that he knew how valued she was. Melanie chose this job over a higher-paying one, saying that the opportunity to help others was the deciding factor.

Even many of the fast-food and retail workers talked about their customers as being the best part of their jobs. Jackie, who worked for the same retail chain for many years, had long-time customers whom she knew well. LaVonda, a fast-food worker, and Sally, who made the rounds of several discount retail stores, told us that, despite having to deal with rude customers, they enjoyed the fact that every day they got to meet people and talk with them. Both characterized themselves as "outgoing" and "social."

Of course, jobs that require a lot of interaction with the public, particularly paying customers, can also be stressful and not at all rewarding. About a third of the participants in our qualitative sample were employed in what might be considered very stereotypical low-wage jobs—as fast-food workers, custodians or housekeepers, or cashiers in retail chains. Many of these women reported that rude or angry customers could make their jobs extremely unpleasant, or, in a few instances, dangerous. Several fast-food workers reported that it was not at all uncommon for them to be sworn at over a mistake in an order or in a drive-through line that wasn't moving fast enough. LaVonda, a veteran of fast-food work, reported that incidents like this happened to her about "four times a week." Mishon had to call the police when hotel guests at the establishment where she cleaned rooms made threats against her or her fellow employees. Kelly, another fast-food worker, threw french fries at a customer who was shouting profanities at her. Kelly's rationale was that she "wasn't paid enough to be called a bitch." Although Kelly later realized that she was very lucky to escape the incident without losing her job (or having charges pressed against her), dealing with situations like these for a wage slightly above the federal minimum made her feel quite stressed.

When we first started developing the WES survey instruments, a popular notion, and one held by numerous welfare-to-work service providers with whom we spoke, was that many welfare recipients were like Kelly. That is, they did not know how to control their tempers and lacked understanding of other basic workplace rules. When I was conducting a study of welfare and welfare-to-work office practices, I often was told that "the problem with welfare recipients is that they get a job and then their car breaks down and they don't call in and they lose their job." Alternatively, "They don't understand that their boss *can* tell them what to do, and the first time they don't want to do something they talk back to their supervisor and get fired." Ruby Payne, the founder of Aha! Process, Inc., has built a successful business by training welfare agency staff and workers at private companies, including Cascade Engineering in Michigan, about methods for working effectively with children and adults from the "poverty culture." In her book A *Framework for Understanding Poverty* (1998), Payne lists characteristics of people who are from this background. Payne contends that the poor are more likely to get mad and quit jobs because they prioritize current feelings over longer-term ramifications; sometimes are not emotionally reserved when angry but rather say exactly what is on their minds; periodically need time off or arrive late to work due to family emergencies; and view organizations, and the people who represent them, as basically dishonest (p. 76).[2]

We decided to test our WES respondents' knowledge of various workplace behavior norms by asking them in the first survey in 1997 if the following would be a serious problem: to be late to work by more than five minutes, miss a day of work without notifying a supervisor, make personal phone calls at work, lose one's temper at work, take a longer-than-scheduled break without first getting permission, not correct a problem pointed out by one's supervisor, not get along with one's supervisor, leave work early without permission, and refuse to do tasks that were outside one's job description. Our expectation was that significant proportions of the sample would think that violating at least some of these norms was "not a problem." Summing up all nine of these workplace norms, we found that only 4.7 percent knew just four or fewer of these norms. That is, less than 5 percent conformed to the expectations of many welfare-to-work providers by thinking that violating most of these norms might be acceptable in the workplace. By contrast, 82 percent of the sample agreed that, on at least seven of these nine items, acting in such a way would be a serious problem. One might plausibly argue that a couple of the items we asked about—in particular, not getting along with one's supervisor and making personal calls at work—might *not* be a serious problem. Supervisors and their employees do not necessarily need to be friends in order to get a job done, and, in many workplaces, the occasional and brief personal phone call is permitted.

However, in subsequent surveys we asked about respondents' actual behavior on the job, and we found that, despite knowing that certain behaviors were not appropriate at work, at any given survey wave, about half of the sample had violated at least one of the norms, although the proportion fell to about 42 percent at the last survey wave (2003). Women who were not currently working reported more past violations than those currently working. For example, and as shown in Table 5.2, in 1999 about 55 percent of workers reported that they had done at least one of the following: been late to work by more than five minutes, lost their temper at work, taken a longer break than scheduled, had problems getting along with a supervisor, left work earlier than usual, refused to do tasks outside their job description, or missed a day of work. The mean number of work norm violations for currently working respon-

Table 5.2 Violations of Work Norms among WES Respondents on Current or Most Recent Job as Measured in 1999 (n = 536)

Violation	Nonworkers (%)	Workers (%)
Late more than 5 minutes	21.6	25.5
Lost temper with rude customer	7.8	7.4
Took longer break than scheduled	7.8	3.4
Problem getting along with supervisor	13.7	6.0
Left work earlier than usual	2.9	1.4
Refused to do tasks outside job description	2.0	2.8
Missed a day of work	63.7	41.1
Any violation	76.5	55.0
Mean number of violations	1.2	0.5

SOURCE: Author's tabulations from WES data.

dents was 0.5. However, for those not currently working (and whose answers reflected the circumstances at their most recent job), the mean number of violations was 1.2, and more than 76 percent reported at least one violation on their last job.

Missing a day of work was the most common "problem" behavior, particularly for those not currently working, as was lateness, both for the working and nonworking. Women who were not working at the time of the survey were also quite likely to report past problems getting along with their supervisors. For some of these women, we might guess that they quit or were fired because of such difficulties. Although we cannot make a definitive causal link, in large part because we did not ask such questions in the WES survey, the stories told by women in the qualitative interviews might lead one to wonder if the strains experienced by women in their jobs, coupled with the relatively low pay they received, contributed to having problems with their supervisors, losing their tempers, skipping work, or otherwise engaging in some of the behaviors they knew were problematic. In addition to the climate at work, being a single mother itself often added to stress levels.

WORKING, WITH CHILDREN

Olivia had been employed at a bank for about seven years when we talked to her in 2004. She worked various shifts, sometimes 8 a.m. to 5 p.m., sometimes noon until 9 p.m. Part of the reason that her schedule varied so much was that her particular job was in the bank's call center, which was open beyond standard business hours. Olivia told us that her job was quite stressful. She, along with 200 co-workers, sat in a room divided by large cubicles organized by the department they represented. Olivia handled corporate customers and fielded calls from several hundred individuals a day. Throughout the room were electronic signs, telling the staff how many clients were waiting to have their calls taken, with the number constantly blinking. Most of Olivia's calls lasted less than 10 minutes, although she reported that many inquiries, such as those requesting loan applications, required her to process paperwork that had to be handled expeditiously. The time pressures of this job were great, and, like many of her counterparts in our study, Olivia noted that her customers were not always pleasant when on the phone with her. Another significant strain of this job was that Olivia could not depend upon a regular schedule week to week, and typically her hours varied a lot within a week. Olivia complained that this situation threw off her sleep, but, more importantly, she believed that a set schedule would allow her more time to spend with her children. She often worked through dinner and lamented the fact that her children ate hot dogs on those nights.

Not surprisingly, a satisfactory schedule was the third-most commonly cited characteristic of a good job. While women's definitions of a "good" schedule varied, a common theme was the desire for hours of work compatible with family responsibilities. Specifically, women believed that good jobs enable them to be home for their children when necessary or when they wanted to be. As Mishon, a single mother, said, "If you can get a job that's kind of flexible, that's good because, especially those that are single parents, like myself, you never know when a child will get hurt at school. Or you never know, something happens at school and you have to leave, or you might have to, you know, go in that morning with your child to school to talk to the principal or teacher or something." Olivia experienced this firsthand. She told us that recently her son had gotten into a fight at school, and she was called to retrieve him. Her supervisor, a younger man without children, insisted that she find someone else to pick up her son so that she could finish her shift. Olivia told us this story when we asked her whether or not she had had any negative experiences on her job. In Olivia's mind, this stood out as the worst. To her, as for so many of our mothers, children come first, and an ideal job is one where that sentiment is shared.

Maylene, in her late twenties with two children and an ill mother, believed no job was so good that it would come before her family responsibilities. She told us that if put in a situation like Olivia's she would quit. Indeed, Maylene had recently left a job because she believed that the employer wanted her to "choose between my family or them." In her words, her family is "who I take care of on a regular basis. Any one of them gets sick, I don't care what I'm doing—you don't let me leave, I'm leaving anyway. Because this is my family, and you ain't going to stop me from doing what I have to do with my family because you want me to stay and work the rest of my hours." When we interviewed her, Maylene was receiving payment from the state to care for her ill grandmother, an ideal situation in one sense, since she would never need to worry about leaving work to tend her grandmother—her grandmother *was* her work. On the other hand, Maylene was being paid the equivalent of $2.50 an hour for her efforts.

For at least seven women in this study, the schedule of their current jobs was one of the primary factors that motivated them to apply for the position in the first place. For example, Johnetta's job at the auto factory was initially offered to her as four 10-hour shifts a week, leaving her with Fridays, Saturdays, and Sundays free. She said that, with this schedule, she was able to plan meetings with teachers and doctors' appointments for Fridays and spend the weekends relaxing with her sons. However, her schedule subsequently changed, and she was working second shift, five days a week, when we interviewed her. Anita and Sally, both of whom had typical low-wage jobs at a fast-food chain and a large discount retailer, respectively, applied for their jobs because of their flexible schedules. While places like Wal-Mart, Burger King, McDonald's, and similar businesses receive attention for their lack of flexibility and other offerings that might make a workplace more family friendly, Anita and Sally told us that they had friends and relatives already working at particular stores who reported that the management was sympathetic to women with children. However, one can imagine that their employers' willingness to work around their schedules would have limits. In fact, Anita was planning on quitting her job for the summer once her son got out of school, because she anticipated too many problems with child care, given the type she could afford.

When asked what they liked best about their current jobs, the schedule was the second-most-common answer, after helping and working with people. Most of the issues around schedules had to do with spending time with children. Many women worked hours that coincided with their children's school days, or at a minimum, allowed them to send their children to school in the morning or to be there in the afternoon when they returned. A number of women held views similar to those of Mishon, who was disdainful of women who sent their kids "off to granny." Lorraine, in her mid-thirties with three school-aged children, previously had her children stay with her sister while she worked evenings. Her sister never monitored the children's homework as Lorraine always had, leading Lorraine to believe that only she could provide the kind of supervision they needed. Lorraine hoped to get a better-paying job than her current one as a janitor in a hospital. Her lack of a high school diploma, she believed, held her back, and she was determined that her children would get more education.

DO WOMEN HAVE "GOOD" JOBS?

In the previous chapter, employment advancement was considered in terms of receiving an hourly wage that would put the average single-parent family over the federal poverty line, although, as discussed, this narrow definition does not match women's characterization of good jobs. My colleagues Johnson and Corcoran developed a more comprehensive description of a good job, which was one paying at least $7 an hour with health insurance or $8.50 without, in a job that is full time (or part time if the part-time decision is voluntary). Using this definition, just under half of the women we interviewed in depth, 15 total, had good jobs, and 16 did not, while one was unemployed. Only 29 percent of the individuals in the full WES survey sample were working in good jobs in 2003.

Yet, the majority of the women we talked to, 23 of the 32, believed that their jobs were good ones; a few women had mixed opinions, while only two thought their jobs were bad. Despite the high prevalence of various difficulties, including discrimination and harassment at the workplace, and despite challenges in dealing with supervisors, co-workers, and customers, most women, even those working at very low wages, were adamant that they had good jobs. Kathleen, who left higher-paying employment to pursue a career in day care, acknowledged that many people would think her job was bad: she was barely paid above minimum wage and dealt with "screaming" children all day. For a change, however, she was doing something she loved, and to her that was extremely important.

After interviewing Vivian, a 43-year-old mother of three who looked much older than her years, I imagined that she would tell me in no uncertain terms that she had a bad job. Vivian had been working at a family-owned restaurant for five years. She disliked her two supervisors immensely and believed that many of her co-workers were "backstabbers." She hadn't had a raise in several years, was paid $7.25 an hour, had no benefits, and each month her hours were reduced further, to the point where she could hardly count on half-time employment. Yet, when I asked her if she had a good job, she immediately said yes. I was surprised and asked her to explain a bit more. She said, "I'm my own boss and they leave me alone." Vivian valued her autonomy, and further, after five years on the job, had mastered all of the tasks associated with her work. As such, she was generally left alone to manage the restaurant's salad bar. For a woman who admittedly battled depression, this sense of command and mastery was likely very important to her.

Kelly initially took a fast-food job as a way to make some additional money and to supplement her earnings as a security guard. When she was laid off from the latter position, she increased her hours at the fast-food restaurant. Although an opportunity to return to the security job, which paid much more than fast food, had presented itself, Kelly was leaning toward not returning to her "good" job and instead staying in the lower-paying one. Kelly had started taking classes toward an associate's degree, and the managers at the fast-food restaurant were very willing to work with her to set a schedule around her courses. She greatly doubted that the security company would do the same. Janelle, a housekeeper in a hotel, took the view held by the Work First program, that any job is a good job and the only bad job is no job at all. Reportedly happy where she was, Janelle only wished that her job offered her benefits. If that were the case, then she "would have the best job!"

Clearly, a number of the women we interviewed, and many in the larger WES survey, had advanced and were in "good" jobs, based on the definition tied to the poverty line. Six of the women we talked to in depth were making more than $10 an hour in 2003. Given that most of these individuals worked full time, full year, and only had a couple of children, on average, their earnings put them well over the poverty line. However, as noted earlier, most women, both those doing well and those working for lower wages, had fairly modest expectations about what they deserved in terms of employment. For some, low hopes about what their current jobs could offer seemed to translate into dim prospects about their futures more generally. Other women had very clear plans, and some were even taking steps to achieve the goals they had laid out for themselves. All women, though, noted real challenges to fulfilling their aspirations. In the next chapter, I further examine women's pathways to employment advancement, taking special note of the real and perceived hindrances to upward mobility and of the trade-offs women made to balance work and family.

Notes

1. Under AFDC, families leaving welfare due to increased earnings or greater child support were eligible for Transitional Medicaid Assistance (TMA), as long as they had received Medicaid in at least three of the previous six months before exiting. The delinking of welfare and Medicaid changed entry into the TMA program. The potential loss of Medicaid, not welfare, due to earnings or increased child support is now the event triggering entry into TMA. However, the receipt of Medicaid in three of the prior six months is still necessary to receive TMA, so that families in which the adult finds a job or increases her wage quickly may not qualify. See Mann (1999) for more details.
2. Payne (1998), it is important to note, makes these claims based upon her observations from years teaching school and from her experience with her husband's family, who were from a "poverty culture." She does not draw upon empirical data.

6
Challenges to Advancement among Former Welfare Recipients

"A job, a better job, a career . . . " The catchphrase of Michigan's Work First program implies that once welfare recipients gain a toehold on the employment ladder and continue to accumulate work experience, their wages will rise and their jobs will be better. However, the appropriateness of this metaphor in summing up welfare recipients' employment trajectories is open to question. Research like the WES demonstrates that many welfare recipients have significant and sometimes multiple barriers to employment. The more such challenges a recipient has, the less likely she is to work at all, let alone climb the rungs of the employment ladder. While a good number of recipients do work, as we see in Chapter 2, much of that employment is unsteady, perhaps disrupting their wage progression. Even among those who are employed steadily, not all experience wage growth; recall that about a quarter of the WES sample stayed in "poverty-wage jobs" over the entire survey period or were in them at the end (see Table 3.3).

However, the conceptual models of welfare recipients' employment paths and of the influential factors leave out one very important consideration: the calculations that women themselves make when thinking about what jobs to take. As we see in the previous chapter, the characteristics that women believe make a job good or bad go far beyond the pay and benefits. In order to obtain more insight into the decision-making process around employment and advancement, I again look to the qualitative interview data, examining the following questions: 1) How do women perceive their own opportunities for and challenges to employment advancement? 2) What do they think about the place of education and training as it relates to upward mobility? 3) What role do family responsibilities play in women's decisions about when to take new jobs and when to participate in educational programs?

OPPORTUNITIES FOR ADVANCEMENT

As discussed earlier, descriptions of opportunity within the low-wage labor market often invoke colorful metaphors, in particular, the characterizations of jobs as "dead-end." However, many women we interviewed did not view their jobs in this way. When we asked them whether or not opportunities for advancement existed in their current positions, more than half believed that they could progress. Nine women noted that within their companies a lower-level employee could be promoted to supervisor. Indeed, three of the women interviewed—LaVonda, Mishon, and Olivia—pointed to their own promotions as evidence of opportunities for upward mobility in their places of work. Of course, perceptions of advancement are always relative. Mishon's promotion to a supervisor of housekeeping in the hotel in which she worked did not seem to have any raise in pay attached to it, and she continued to make barely above the minimum wage.

Offers of promotion were not always accepted, however. Other women said that, while supervisor positions were available, and some had been offered this job, they did not want to move up into this role. Several said that the extra tasks and responsibilities associated with supervision were not worth the relatively small increase in pay. Other women contended that being a supervisor entailed giving up certainty over one's schedule. Caroline, a registered nurse, had been asked by the hospital's management on numerous occasions to take on a supervisory position, but she always declined. She told us, "I've been asked to take [the supervisor job] at least six times by management. Other people on the floor, my co-workers, they keep encouraging me to take that job because they feel I would be a very good unit manager, that I could run a unit. I don't want to do that, and the only reason I don't want to do it—because it would be an advancement in pay [and] it's day hours, which is good because I could work, like, 8 to 4, the latest I'd be out is 4:30—but the bad part about it is you have to be on call, and I don't like the on-call thing. Because if another nurse calls in and that's your day to be on call or that's your weekend to be on call, no matter what shift it is, you have to get up and go in and cover. So that's the disadvantage to that. Other than that, I probably would take the position, because like I said it would be a great advancement in pay. But I just can't get used to the idea of being on call because I believe in my time and when I'm off, I'm off. I don't want to get up and come in and work for nobody unless I choose to. I don't want it to be a mandatory thing that I have to."

Quite a few women we interviewed told us that there were career ladders within the organization, but various considerations kept them from applying for upper-level jobs. For example, Jackie said that in order to take a current opening for a higher-paying job, she would have to commute 35 minutes each way to another store owned by the grocery chain for which she worked. Compared to her current commute of 10 minutes, this trip was much too long. Also, driving to the more distant store would mean that Jackie would not be around to see her daughter off to school in the morning. Other women noted that their workplaces offered them opportunities to participate in training that would lead to promotions or that their place of work would reimburse them for participation in outside education and training programs. Olivia, who worked for a bank, had gone through numerous classes offered by her company, allowing her to progress through the ranks and to take on additional responsibilities. Tia, a clerical employee in a hospital, was studying to become a physical therapist. The hospital reimbursed her for tuition. A couple of women, though, stated that while these opportunities existed in their places of employment, they had not taken advantage of them.

Several women reported that any opportunities for continued advancement were limited by their lack of seniority within the organization or by their level of education. That is, the organization posted job openings, and personnel could apply for higher-paying positions, but only after being employed for some length of time (two years in one case), with consideration for new positions based in part on seniority. For others, moves higher up the ladder required specific skills or certifications that they did not have. Cherie, a pharmacy technician, said that the only opportunity for a higher-paying job within the store where she worked was as a pharmacist, a job requiring a college education as well as additional schooling. While Cherie had completed high school as well as extra training programs, she could not advance beyond her current position, which paid just under $10 an hour.

In the last chapter we saw how many women experienced stress on the job, including problems with overbearing supervisors who sometimes played favorites or engaged in discriminatory behavior. While these experiences certainly contributed to unpleasant workplaces, at least some women believed that favoritism within the organization was a limiting factor for advancement. Denise, an employee in a group home for the elderly and mentally disabled, was very clear that her opportunities to move up were quite constrained. When asked if she might ever get promoted to manager, she said, "This is a family-run type business place, so you got to know somebody. If you don't know nobody, you ain't going nowhere. If they cousin or son or girlfriend come working for the place, they'll be a manager in three months. Never been a manager, never had any experience, never worked in a group home, and this is the type of thing you have to worry about." Other women told similar stories about the lack of promotion opportunities in family-run businesses. Some said that the only employees who moved up were those who were particular favorites of the bosses. Ellen, who worked for a clothing store, said, "I had a chance to go for the assistant manager job and she [my supervisor] made sure she handpicked who she wanted, which I don't think is fair. I think the person who is qualified should have got the job, because this new assistant manager can't cut it. See, I'm doing more than she [the assistant manager] is. The assistant manager is just incapable of doing what we do." Whether or not these perceptions were true, many women believed that within their current jobs, upward mobility was elusive.

We also asked the 32 women we interviewed to assess whether or not they had advanced over the last five years (the time period roughly corresponding to the WES survey data collection). We kept this question rather open ended; for example, we wanted women to tell us about how they perceived their own employment trajectories and to talk about the factors they considered in making judgments about their progression. Nearly two-thirds (21) of qualitative respondents believed that they had advanced, at least in some aspects, while 9 believed they had not.[1] However, women's answers about whether or not they had moved ahead were filled with discrepancies. For example, 8 of the women who told us that they had advanced cited increased pay and promotions as the reasons behind their answers. However, among these 8, 4 had negative or little wage growth. Sheila, a 39-year-old mother of two, had recently taken an assembly job at a company that produced automobile parts. Although at first glance, one might imagine that a manufacturing job would be a big step up from her previous position as an aide in a nursing home, Sheila's hourly wage only increased by 50¢ between

2001 and 2003 and was roughly the same as it had been in 1997. However, the 50¢ increase was noteworthy to Sheila, who also saw further opportunities for adding to her paycheck by learning to operate different types of machinery. It is also very likely that taking an auto-parts manufacturing job was a symbolic move upward for Sheila, even if the pay raise was not that large. Sheila said that she had always hoped to get a factory job, once very prevalent in the community, but now dwindling in number.

Others noted that they had gained new skills or had taken on additional responsibilities. Amanda started off performing routine clerical tasks at minimum wage for a small law firm but moved up to be the office manager. While her pay had risen to about $10 an hour, she still lacked health insurance and other benefits. However, she believed that the increased responsibility was noteworthy, saying, "I've advanced as far as getting more responsibility. We have to look at it [advancement] in different terms for me. So I've advanced in the level of responsibility I've been given . . . Pay—I'm sure that if they could afford to pay me more, they would. I truly think that the reason I don't get paid more is because we're small and because it's what they can afford to keep the office going." A dispatcher for a local transportation company that primarily served the elderly and disabled, Melanie turned down a promotion to a management position because it would have removed her from day-to-day interactions with customers. Her hourly wage remained mostly flat, but she still believed that she had advanced: "Even though I didn't take the pay, it's like I have something else higher. I guess just—I call it my little old ladies. You know, they're just—I mean, my little old crew. That's more important to me, seeing them get to their appointments." As noted in the previous chapter, Melanie told us that she took her current job over another, higher-paying, offer, because the dispatcher's position gave her an opportunity to help others.

Nine women were unequivocal about their lack of advancement. Their median wage growth over the six and a half years was about 2 percent total, or, in the words of Lorraine, a housekeeper in a hospital, "Just a few nickels and dimes more, that's all." Most of these women recognized that their pay had not increased. Some felt frustrated that they were doing the same type of work and that their jobs had not changed, but at least a couple put partial blame upon themselves. Toni, a mother of three teenagers, worked nine months out of the year for a local school, providing help in the lunchroom and other teacher's aide–related tasks. While believing this job to be ideal because the schedule allowed her to be at home during the same times as her children, she acknowledged that it had been at a cost. She said to us, "I've been at a standstill with my job, and some of it is my own—it is my fault because I could be doing something else, but I choose not to, like bus driving. I could have made time to be a bus driver [by taking training classes] and make more money and have my benefits." Lorraine, a housekeeper, had applied for several different positions within the hospital and was passed over for all of them. She blamed her lack of education, saying, "It's like I'm still stuck in the same position that I am, you know. I think they still looking for high school graduates and up, and I just ain't that."

FURTHER EDUCATION AND TRAINING

Lorraine's comment about employers wanting workers with high school diplomas and about the implications of her lacking a diploma on advancement raises the issue about the effect of further education and training on upward mobility. Advanced degrees and technical skills are of increasing value in our labor market (Murnane and Levy 1996). The multivariate analyses showed a relationship between lack of a high school education and downward employment transitions; not graduating or not having a GED increased the probability of moving into a poverty-wage job after first holding an above-poverty-wage job (see Figure 3.4). Nearly half of the women we interviewed in depth believed that their single largest challenge to advancing further was their insufficient education. Yet, state welfare systems moved away from assisting recipients in obtaining further schooling, even prior to the 1996 welfare reform. Once the law's work requirements—and restrictions in allowing educational activities to count toward meeting the requirements—went into effect, few states provided help to recipients in going to school or participating in vocational training activities.

To the extent that women obtained additional training during the time they were in our study, they did it on their own and often while they were working. Table 6.1 shows the proportion of WES survey respondents who, between 1997 and 2003, participated in any of the fol-

Table 6.1 Participation in Education and Training, 1997–2003

Activity	All WES wave 5 respondents ($n = 536$)	Wave 5 respondents without diploma/ GED in 1997 ($n = 160$)	Wave 5 respondents with a high school diploma/GED in 1997($n = 376$)	Qualitative respondents ($n = 32$)
	Participation (%)			
GED/high school completion	7.5	20.0***	2.1	9.4
Vocational training	29.7	27.5	30.6	15.6
College	22.0	4.4	29.5***	25.0
Any education or training, 1997–2003	57.5	51.3	60.1*	53.1

NOTE: *Difference between wave 5 respondents without a high school diploma/GED and with a high school diploma/GED is significant at $p < 0.10$. ***Difference between wave 5 respondents without a high school diploma/GED and with a high school diploma/GED is significant at $p < 0.01$. Percentages in a particular column will not equal the proportion ever participating in education or training because it is possible that some respondents engaged in multiple activities.
SOURCE: Author's tabulations from WES data.

lowing: GED or high school completion programs, vocational training programs, and/or work toward an associate's, bachelor's, or graduate degree. The bottom row of the table shows the percentage who participated in any of these educational/training activities.

As seen in the first column of data, more than half of all respondents in the survey reported that they had participated in some educational or training activity. Just under 30 percent enrolled in a vocational program or class, and 22 percent had taken college courses, while a much smaller number, 7.5 percent, participated in GED or high school completion activities. Important differences exist, though, between the types of activities and the educational attainment of the respondents when first surveyed in 1997. For example, and as would be expected, participation in GED preparation activities was much more common among those without a high school diploma, with 20 percent of those without this credential in 1997 reporting that they had taken steps toward obtaining a GED.[2] Among those who finished high school, additional training is fairly evenly split between vocational training and college classes. Although not shown in the table, taking college classes was more common among those who already had some postsecondary education in 1997 (42.4 percent of the 172 respondents with additional education) compared to those who had finished high school only (18.6 percent of the 204 respondents completing high school). This suggests that those who were already more educationally advantaged were the ones most likely to attend college, although no significant differences appear by attendance at a vocational program. However, what the data do not show is completion of a program or a degree.

The last column of the table displays participation in these activities among qualitative sample members as reported in the surveys. However, some of these activities were missed. In total, 21 of the 32 women, when interviewed in depth, reported that they had engaged in some form of education and training activities. However, it is important to remember that few of these 32 women lacked high school diplomas when first interviewed in 1997, so it is not surprising that just 3 women participated in GED preparation activities. One of these women, Sierra, a 30-year-old mother of three, started a GED class but eventually dropped out of the program. Money to pay for child care was the major problem. "Like I said, I really didn't have the money to pay a babysitter, and when you got kids, it costs money, you know, even to leave them for someone to watch them for a few hours. So, I just really didn't have the money to do it anymore."

Five of the women we spoke to in depth had previously reported in the survey that they had participated in vocational training activities, or, as the survey asked, "training for a specific job." Further examination of the interview data indicates that much of this training consisted of seminars or classes specific to the employer. For example, several women who worked in food-related jobs were required to take food-safety classes, while others in the health field were required to be certified in CPR. While the skills and certifications achieved through these classes may help women get other, similar jobs, it is unlikely that this type of knowledge will lead to promotions or higher-paying employment elsewhere.

Eight women had attended college during the study period, and another woman had just enrolled when we interviewed her. Like those in the larger WES sample, these eight individuals tended to have completed high school and already had some postsecondary education under their belts when the study first started following them in late 1997.

Nevertheless, actual completion of these programs was slow going, as might be expected with their other commitments to work and family. Among the nine, only Caroline, a registered nurse, and Marie, a law enforcement officer, had finished their course work and received degrees. Another common trait shared by women who attended college was that most had boyfriends, husbands, or family members whom they could call upon for help. Marie, who had a child as a teenager, was a talented athlete who received a track-and-field scholarship to a school out of state. However, her athletic eligibility ran out before she completed her degree, and Marie found herself back in Michigan and on welfare. Within a short time, she was able to transfer to another four-year institution and eventually graduate, ending up as one of the highest-paid women in our study. Marie credited the support she received from her parents, which included babysitting for her daughter while she was in classes and studying, as crucial for her being able to get a bachelor's degree.

Regina, Amanda, and Tia were currently enrolled in programs. Regina was taking her college courses online, which allowed her more flexibility in her schedule. Nevertheless, she received significant support from both her cohabiting partner and her other family members. Her boyfriend helped with the bills, her father bought her a car, her grandmother watched her children, and her mother provided "constant moral support . . . telling me I can do it, reassuring me." Kathleen, who was about to return to school full time, felt financially secure in leaving her job as a day care provider because her husband worked in construction with a very good salary. Tia, although recently married, did not have such support and believed that her grades suffered as a result. She emphasized that her children's education came before hers, saying, "You've got to make sure they're doing good in school. If I've got to drop what I'm doing at school and miss a class to make sure they're getting what they need in school, that's the challenge." Tia was making mostly Cs in her own classes and worried that her grade point average would not be high enough to get into the next stage of the training program.

Even if welfare program administrators downplayed the role of education in employment advancement, most women we interviewed believed education was essential in that respect. Further, most made a sharp distinction between degree and other types of educational programs. Before enrolling in an associate's program, Kathleen had earlier completed a certificate in medical technology. In the end, she said that the certificate did not help her advance because she believed employers give an associate's degree more weight when making hiring decisions. She said, "It's the associate's degree. Yeah, my sister called it something—the initiative to stay for two years—where when she hires people she wants them to go to college because they know they'll last and they stuck it out, so she looks at that [an associate's degree] more than she looks at a certificate, cause that's in and out, you're out of there. Which is how I looked at it, but now I don't cause now I wish I would have done the associate's."

Women who engaged in vocational training programs tended to have mixed evaluations of their usefulness. While the majority who participated believed that training was useful, for the most part this was because they thought it helped them perform their current jobs better, not because it opened up new opportunities for them. The assessment of LaVonda, a fast-food worker, is typical of this. She had taken a number of classes related to food preparation that were offered by the local health department. She said, "It [the class] helped me on my job . . . to know more about the food—the safeties and the precautions on food, 'cause foods are supposed to be a certain temperature, and all-raw foods can't be mixed with ready-to-eat foods, stuff like that."

Furthering their education was a goal of more than half of the women we interviewed, although we detected considerable variation in terms of the drive to do this. For example, as noted, a number of women were enrolled in programs, while several others had researched the various schools and offerings available in the area. Shanice was very close to completing her associate's degree when we talked to her and was starting to look into bachelor's programs. Other women knew that their lack of credentials or skills was holding them back and believed that they should return to school. As Denise, a nurse's aide, said, "If you don't have a high school diploma or some kind of degree, you're going to be cleaning up or cleaning somebody up all your life." However, when pressed to articulate the steps they were taking to achieve this goal, the individuals did not know how they would go back to school or cited real barriers to furthering their education.

Lorraine, a single mother of two, is a good illustration of these challenges. Lorraine talked at length about how bad experiences in high school made it difficult for her to want to enroll in a GED program. She said, "I think it was my 9th grade year I left [Michigan], and I went to Chicago, and the credits was different here than they was there . . . I had finished the 10th grade, I went to the 11th grade, and I happened to see my report card this particular day, and you know how you had to have so many credits to graduate? I looked at my credits and I'm like, God, I don't have that many credits! . . . So come to find out when I left Michigan and came to Chicago they had made me start all over and I didn't know that." Lorraine said that she was particularly hurt that her mother never went to the school to try to talk with officials about getting her credits from Michigan accepted. In the end, she dropped out at 16 and shortly afterward became pregnant with her first child.

A few years later, Lorraine enrolled in a computer training program but found her confidence greatly shaken. "At the computer school I had to do this paper. I wrote this paper and I thought to myself, 'I did real good.' You know, I took my time. I end up getting a C and that kinda disappointed me. I'm like, 'Wait a minute, I put all this time, and wrote this paper and did this and that, and I looked through the books and I tried to use the right words and this is all I get!' See, that's a downfall I have, that goes back to saying that I never had anybody to really support me, and to say, 'Lorraine, you can do it.'"

Age presented at least a perceived challenge for some women. For Ellen, who was in her late thirties, the thought of having to do math after being out of school for 20 years was quite daunting. When we met with her, she was contemplating starting an apprentice program at a local manufacturing company. However, she would have to take a test upon completion of the apprenticeship in order to be hired as a full-time employee. She showed the study guide to Amber, the interviewer, saying, "I haven't had none of this. I'm dumbfounded here . . . sometimes I feel like it's just too late [to go back to school]." Additionally, Ellen noted that, as she had aged, her health problems had increased. Several years earlier she had had a heart attack, which lowered her energy level. While she professed a desire to return to school (over and above the apprentice program), she doubted that she could physically handle the demands of work, school, and family.

Chapter 2 documents the high prevalence of certain personal and family challenges that many have conventionally called "barriers to employment." Ostensibly, some of these impediments could be removed through participation in education and training. For example, a woman with no high school diploma and limited work experience might see her labor market prospects improve if she were able to complete a vocational program that provided some on-the-job training. However, similar to employment barriers, other constraints might interfere with going back to school. Women like Ellen who had physical limitations may not have the vigor to go to work and to school. Individuals with mental health problems may likewise lack the energy to participate in school, or, as was true for Lorraine, may be plagued with doubts about their ability to succeed in the classroom. Women with learning disabilities, particularly if undiagnosed or untreated, may not be able to function in traditional academic settings.

Other women had thought about returning to school, but demands on the household's income made them hesitant to do so. Johnetta was trying to put aside money so that she could take classes and obtain her real estate license. However, her son was attending a four-year, private college, and she did not believe that she had extra funds to pursue training for herself. Like Ellen, Johnetta worried that her health (a thyroid condition) would prevent her from working and going to school at the same time. Wendy was waiting for her children and stepchildren to finish their high school and postsecondary education before pursuing her own interests. Not only would this free up money, but her responsibilities as a parent would be lessened.

Concerns about their children's well-being were another main reason that women put off participating in education and training. Amanda, an office manager of a law firm, represents this struggle. She said, "My choices are to take night classes and not be around the kids, which I don't like. They're teenagers—they need me at home now more than they ever did. My son's moved out, I have daughters. My youngest has a boyfriend now, so I don't want to be one of those moms and then complain later on, well, what happened? If I take classes during the day, I'm missing work, which is my paycheck, so I can't do that because my paychecks are lower. I can't do that."

This tension between motherhood and career advancement opportunities, whether it be decisions to return to school or choices women make about upward movement on the job, emerged as perhaps the most striking common feature across interviews. Issues of work-family balance receive much attention in the popular media, with the coverage, as in the *New York Times'* articles cited at the beginning of this book, typically focusing on middle- and upper-middle-class women and the decisions they make about pursuing careers versus spending time with children. However, we found numerous examples of this same tension among lower-wage, working single mothers.

CHOICES ABOUT ADVANCEMENT AND THE ROLE OF MOTHERHOOD

Juggling employment and parenting is never an easy proposition, particularly for single parents. Trying to add another commitment, such as school, is often more than can be managed. For the vast majority of women we interviewed, some sort of balance had been struck in their lives, and many seemed unwilling to risk disrupting their schedules by returning to school and/or taking a different job. In large part this was because of their children.

For some women, decisions about employment advancement were tied to concerns that have been previously articulated in the literature about work and welfare (Edin and Lein 1997). For example, one woman worried about what might happen if she was not at home to monitor her children's behavior, particularly since her oldest child had gotten into trouble when unsupervised. Toni, a teacher's aide, believed it was very important to have a work schedule that matched her children's. She said, "My kids are teenagers, and having teenagers, I think a parent needs to be at home when they're home because they get carried away . . . I experienced that already with my oldest son, so I don't want to make that same mistake with these two." Other women feared that, without their supervision at home, their teenage daughters would become pregnant.

Problems with child care, including finding reliable and affordable services, have also been commonly cited concerns in studies focusing on women in the low-wage labor market. While child care problems forced Sierra to drop out of a GED preparation class, for most women in the qualitative study, arranging child care was not an issue. In fact, most women were like Toni and had school-age and teenage children. Despite not needing formal child care, these women expressed a strong wish to spend time with their children and to participate in their activities. This desire sometimes got in the way of further advancement. Jackie did not apply for a promotion because it would mean transferring to a more distant store. She explained how her daughter's activities and schedule played a role in her employment decisions. She said, "If it [the job] was in my store, I probably would [apply], but if it was somewhere else I just can't do it right now because of my nine-year-old . . . I'd have to get up earlier, and I ain't got nobody here to get my daughter, you know . . . And usually I have a lot to deal with . . . I do help out in Girl Scouts, I'm a coleader. My daughter's very, very busy, and it's just like trying to participate in her life and her stuff. She's into this science project—we're so far behind on that. I've got to get that together. And then, like, next week, Saturday, on my day off, I've got to go pick up $700 worth of Girl Scout cookies and put them in my Blazer . . . But, that makes it kind of hard, I mean, working, because there's so much stuff going on in her life and sometimes I can't be at everything, and that kind of upsets me."

Similar to findings in recent work by Edin and Kefalas (2005), my research shows that women place a high value on being a mother. Based on interviews with young women in inner-city neighborhoods, Edin and Kefalas propose that poor women derive much meaning out of life from bearing children, perhaps in large part because, unlike middle-class and upper-middle-class individuals, "rewarding careers and professional identities [are not] . . . available" to them (p. 206). In many ways, the women in our sample are the older sisters of those interviewed by Edin and Kefalas. They are working, and their children are older, but their values have not changed.

Anita, a fast-food employee who had refused promotions to manager, talked about how working too much had a detrimental effect on her friend's children. She said, "It's like these days if you're a single parent and you're the mother that's taking care of the household—like right now, I have a friend and her boyfriend helps out somewhat but not really, so she has to be the breadwinner of the house. And she's doing that, but it's hurting the kids. One of them, who is my godchild, well, she's the same age as my son, she's 7 or 8, but she can barely read. And it's like when her mama get home, she's tired. It's hard for her to spend the time, to take the time out that—I guess that might be somewhat of an excuse, too, for her, but it's like if she wasn't working as hard or didn't have to do as much, maybe she could spend time with her to help with learning how to read things because that's important, that's real important . . . It seems like if she would have had more time then it would have been better for the kids instead of having to go out and do all that [work]. I know we bring things on to ourselves by having kids early and young, but still, you still have to raise your kids rather than [them] raising their selves or somebody else raising them." While recognizing that a choice was made to have children at a younger age and as an unmarried woman, Anita firmly believed that, once children are there, mothers have the responsibility for their well-being.

In fact, one-third of the women we interviewed, when asked about their greatest challenges to further advancement, said that responsibilities to their children prevented them from progressing. A number of women believed that, once their children were grown, they would be able to devote time to themselves and would be able to advance. Amanda, the office manager and mother of three children, represents this view. She said, "A lot of my time that I could devote to education and to work, I choose to spend on my children, and that's temporary. Once the kids are grown, I won't have any real reasons to keep me from growing and moving ahead." Sierra held similar views, noting that her purpose for working now was not to advance but to provide for her children: "Well, it's my family and kids right now. It [work] ain't just for me, basically right now it's for the kids. I'll have my life later. So you know, basically it's the kids for me right now." Of course, putting children before job advancement did mean that, generally, the family's income remained low.

On the other hand, even if they turned down higher-paying jobs, many women were keenly aware of being the sole breadwinner of their families. While they might want to spend more time with their children and had found positions that allowed them greater flexibility to do so, they also knew that ultimately they were responsible for their family's economic and overall well-being. In addition to being the exclusive parent in the house (and in many cases, the sole parent involved in their children's lives), they also were the only person working, the one who paid all of the bills, and who made sure food was in the house and meals were prepared. Several women invoked the same metaphor to describe this situation, saying that they felt an incredible weight on their shoulders, knowing that the full burden of supporting their families fell on them. Barbara, a 32-year-old woman who managed a trucking company, summed up her feelings by saying, "It gets stressful, taking care of everything, being both mom and dad and then having to work."

Perhaps as a result, many women expected their children to help out quite a bit around the house. About a third of all women interviewed, when asked in what ways their family supported them as working mothers, noted that their children did at least some housework. Certain children were reported to play a more significant role in the running of the home. A number of women told us that their children prepared dinner at least some nights during the week. Shanice was one of these individuals; she said that her 14-year-old daughter could cook anything in Shanice's repertoire and frequently had dinner ready when she returned home from her job as a transportation aide.

Despite help from their children, most women reported that the majority of the housework, as well as the cooking, was ultimately their job. Arlie Hochschild (1989) has called this phenomenon the "second shift." As Hochschild notes, the growth of mothers in the paid labor force has generally resulted in women having another load of housework and related chores once their paid job has ended. Denise recognized that she had such a second shift, saying, "You go to work [and] a lot of times you think when you leave work your job is done. But you a mother [and] your first job is done, [but] you've got to go home and do your second job." Also, the expectations of that second job are great. In *The Cultural Contradictions of Motherhood*, Hays (1996) contends that an ideology of motherhood has arisen that stresses "emotionally demanding, financially draining, labor-consuming child rearing" just at the time that women are in the paid labor force in record numbers (p. 4). So, not only does a second shift exist, Hays says, but its demands are even greater. It is not enough to be a parent: Hays says one needs to engage in "intensive mothering," investing in children's needs by providing them opportunities to participate in extracurricular activities and by closely monitoring their development, as many of the women in our study reported to be doing. While Hochschild argues for a more equitable distribution of household labor between men and women, such an arrangement would be of little use to the women in our study. As single parents, no other adult is around to help. Caroline summed up her situation this way: "I don't have that spouse to say, 'Well, honey, you know what, I just can't handle this today. You take care of it.' There's nobody but me to take care of it, I don't have a choice. And that's when it becomes really, really stressful, and there are days where you just want to put your head down and you just feel like crying."

Many women experienced stress not only from their jobs but from the balancing act they were trying to maintain. Caroline was not alone in admitting to having periodic breakdowns or to feeling overwhelmed and very tired. More than a dozen women talked about how "stressed out" they were, trying to manage a full-time job along with being a parent. While having older children often eased the day care problem for many individuals, their sons and daughters were active in sports and other after-school activities. Many mothers also wanted a better life for their children and closely tracked their progress in school. Having a job that allowed time off to attend parent-teacher conferences was very important for a number of the women in our study. Johnetta told us that in addition to her full-time job on the line, she volunteered at least twice a week at her younger son's school so that she could talk with his teachers and see how he was doing. Johnetta's older son was a sophomore at a prestigious private university, and she wanted the same opportunities for his brother. Johnetta herself had never finished college. Mishon, the hotel housekeeper, adamantly told us that "putting my kids in front of me is the most important thing to do," meaning that, even if she was tired from a full day at work, she was still going to be available to take them to basketball practice or cook meals for them. The end result for women like Mishon, though, could be a great deal of stress.[3]

However, women also told us that their children were their primary motivation for going to work and doing well on their jobs. Caroline told us that her children were "my sole purpose in doing everything I've done." Similarly, Regina said that her children gave her "more power to go harder, faster, longer, to be able to provide for them." Johnetta and Marie both had jobs that paid well, but with frequent evening shifts, taking them away from their children. Even though both women would have preferred to spend more time with their families, they said that a primary reason for staying on the job was to make sure their children had a higher quality of life. Johnetta said, "I want to help my son so that he can get a better job [as an adult] so that he won't be struggling in this world like his mother is."

ASPIRATIONS FOR ADVANCEMENT AND HOPES FOR HANGING ON

If children were the focus of the present, what might the future hold? We asked women to talk about where they envisioned they would be and what they would be doing in five years. For most mothers we interviewed, this would be a time at which, to a large extent, their children would be grown and out of the house. Not surprisingly, given the importance the individuals placed on education, returning to school was a plan that more than half of the women had for themselves. The majority of women talked about going to school or completing other training programs. As noted earlier, some women were already slowly accruing credits toward a degree, a few were set to start programs, and additional respondents were actively gathering information on various such opportunities in the area. Other women told us that they wanted to be in school or to have finished school in the next five years, but when pressed for details, had fairly vague notions of what they might do, where they could enroll, and what they might realistically achieve. Sierra, who had in the past tried to take classes toward a GED, still had hopes of getting that certificate. She planned to do this as soon as her youngest child, aged 14, finished school. Beyond this time frame, though, Sierra lacked any firm plans. She wanted to go to college but didn't know if a GED would gain her admission or if she would need a high school diploma.

Most women in our sample could probably be considered quite resourceful on a number of fronts: they were managing households and raising children, typically as the only adult, on relatively low incomes. However, some lacked a sense of what types of programs or services might be available to help them achieve their goals, or they did not want to use these services. When we asked women to tell us what kind of assistance—either from public or private sources—would enable them to fulfill their aspirations, many struggled to answer the question. It seemed as if it were difficult for some women to imagine that government could help them. When pressed, a number mentioned that assistance with paying for education and related expenses would be nice. A couple knew about loan and grant opportunities, such as the Pell Grant, a federal need-based aid program for lower- and middle-income students attending undergraduate institutions. Two women had hopes of opening up their own day care centers and had started researching the types of assistance provided through the "4Cs," the Michigan Community Coordinated Child Care Association, which provides both services and training to child care providers as well as referrals to parents searching for providers.

A more common answer to this question about help was for women to say that the only aid they needed (or perhaps wanted) was from their family and friends. For some, this support manifested itself in concrete services, such as family members who provided child care or friends who were willing to pick up children after school. For other women, the support wanted was emotional. Regina was taking college courses online when we interviewed her, and she cited her mother as providing "constant moral support" and reassurance when she found herself struggling with assignments. Four women very explicitly stated that they did not need any assistance.

Perhaps individuals' prior experience with the welfare system shaped their sense that public entities were not a place to get help. Regarding the benefits of various public assistance programs, including TANF, Work First, Food Stamps, and Medicaid, women's opinions varied, but in general, they were not altogether positive. A common complaint was that getting on public aid "just wasn't worth the hassle" of multiple welfare office appointments and potentially rude treatment by welfare workers. A number of women noted that when welfare reform was implemented, they were sent to participate in the employment program, Work First, even though they already had jobs. It would not be a stretch to imagine that such inefficiency would not inspire great confidence in the public welfare system's ability to help people achieve their goals.

Several women wanted to receive food stamps and/or Medicaid but were told that they earned too much. This was very perplexing to them, since they perceived their wages to be quite low. Jackie complained that now that her older children were teenagers with healthy appetites, she could not keep food in the house at all times. However, with a full-time job paying just under $10 an hour, Jackie was not eligible for the program. Anita, who made barely over the minimum wage and at most could hope to get 20 hours a week of work at her job, also was deemed ineligible because she had married and her husband worked. However, she reported that more than half of his earnings went toward child support for children from previous relationships. When her children were out of school during the summer, Anita quit her job, since child care costs would be more than what she would be able to bring home from a job.

Anita, like many other women, seemed baffled by the requirements of the welfare system. They believed that by working, they were "playing by the rules." Yet, their ability to get any support seemed to go away once they were employed. Anita, at the end of the interview, told us emphatically that she "wanted to talk about FIA" (the Family Independence Agency, the name of Michigan's welfare system at that time). She believed that as soon as recipients started working, benefits were immediately cut. She said, "They cut the food stamps, they cut the money off cause you're making money, and then they'll cut the food stamps when you might just be making enough to pay your bills. And you just have a little bit over, but you have, like, three kids, and these three kids, they got to eat! And it's like, well this bill is not getting paid this month because I have to have food!" Anita thought that the welfare agency should at least provide food stamp benefits to children, if not to working adults.

Like most other states, Michigan allowed welfare recipients to work and retain some TANF benefits. Each month the state permitted recipients to keep the first $200 of earnings plus 20 percent of the remaining earnings before reducing the TANF grant dollar for dollar. However, compared to the policies of other states, Michigan's earned income disregard policy was not especially generous, and a working recipient would be ineligible for welfare unless she worked part time or full time at a very low wage. For example, a single mother with two children who worked 35 hours a week at a job paying $6 an hour would lose eligibility for cash assistance. In contrast, in 24 other states, such a single mother would still qualify for TANF.[4] However, the federal Food Stamp Program is designed to assist low-income working families, regardless of whether or not they receive TANF support. Benefits are provided via a debit card and can be used to purchase food. Eligibility is based on earnings, the number of people who share meals together, and an asset test. A single mother in Michigan with three children should be eligible for at least some food stamp benefits until she makes a little more than $9.30 an hour and works full time.

However, many of our respondents may not have been aware of the rules that allowed them to combine work with benefit receipt. At the third WES survey wave in 1999 we asked respondents a series of questions to determine how much they knew about various welfare regulations, post–welfare reform. Women were asked if they thought that once a recipient got a job, TANF benefits would be ended (the correct answer is no) and the same question about food stamps (again, the correct answer is no). Just under two-fifths (38 percent) of our survey respondents in 1999 believed that women who got a job while on welfare would lose their benefits, and a smaller proportion, 26 percent, thought that food stamp benefits would be ended upon getting a job. Thus, significant segments of the women in our study did not know the welfare rules and may not have sought out benefits for which they may have been eligible.

A smaller number of women in the qualitative portion of the study not only could not think of where they might go for help (or what kind of assistance they might want), they also could not articulate a clear plan for the future. None of these women earned particularly high wages, between $7 and $8 an hour, and all of them expressed a strong dislike for their current jobs. Yet they uniformly seemed at a loss to think about how they might change their current situations. A couple talked vaguely about moving out of the state, noting that Michigan's economy had never completely recovered from the loss of auto manufacturing jobs. Others, such as Sally, a cashier at a large discount retailer, would not consider moving until their children finished school. Until then, she said she didn't have a clue as to what she wanted for her future.

What, then, can policy do to assist women, like many in our study, who want to return to school but do not know how while their children are still at home? What changes could be made in the public assistance system to help lower-income working families, such as those headed by Anita, the fast-food employee, to supplement their wages and to clear up potential misconceptions around eligibility? What role is there for policy to work with women like Sally who are mired in a lower-paying job but see no alternative? Finally, are there ways to encourage more family-friendly practices in lower-wage workplaces or to enact policies that could help all workers better manage their family lives? In the final chapter, I consider these questions.

Notes

1. The remaining two respondents, both of whom were self-employed, had great difficulty answering this question and did not provide an assessment of their overall advancement.
2. As Table 6.1 shows, 2.1 percent ($n = 8$) of those reporting that they had completed high school or a GED in 1997 subsequently reported that they participated in GED or high school completion activities. This could be due to errors in recall, over-reporting of educational attainment at the first interview wave, data entry error, or a combination of these factors.
3. Similar to the rest of the WES sample, in 1997 about 40 percent of the respondents in the qualitative study met the diagnostic screening criteria for any of the following mental health disorders: major depression, posttraumatic stress disorder, generalized anxiety disorder, or social phobia. Over the course of the entire study, 68.4 percent of the sample and 65.6 percent of the qualitative respondents had at least one mental health disorder one or more times.
4. These figures were computed using the "Marriage Calculator" available from the Administration for Children and Families of the U.S. Department of Health and Human Services. We assume that the woman has no assets, no vehicle, receives no child support, and has been on TANF for at least six months. The calculator is available at: http://marriagecalculator.acf.hhs.gov/marriage/calculator.php (accessed April 2008).

7
Policies to Bring Work and Family Back into Balance

When I started this project, I was hoping to uncover differences in the way women made decisions about work and family that might help explain various employment outcomes. The existing literature indicated the importance of certain human capital and personal characteristics in impeding (or assisting) low-skilled workers' advancement prospects. Analysis of the WES data confirmed the findings of much of that research. In Chapter 3 we saw that lack of a high school diploma was associated with downward employment transitions for those starting in above-poverty-wage jobs, low levels of prior work experience increased the predicted probability of subsequent unemployment for those beginning in poverty-wage jobs, and persistent transportation problems increased the likelihood of subsequent unemployment, regardless of the pay level of the starting job.

However, those types of inquiries were not able to shed light upon the actual processes behind movements up or down the employment ladder. What I found, instead, was that the concerns and challenges women articulated cut across employment experiences. Women in poverty-wage jobs talked about issues affecting their ability to move out of the low-income labor market in similar ways that women who were in higher-paying employment discussed challenges to taking even more remunerative positions. Across the pay spectrum, women experienced harassment on the job and what they perceived to be negative working conditions. Nearly all women were concerned about accommodating their children's schedules. Given the commonalities of these experiences, what types of policies could help women like those in the WES sample as they juggle work and family responsibilities?

In this chapter, I review some of the current policies and programs that have been implemented in the hopes of helping the advancement of low-wage workers, and welfare recipients in particular. Given what we learned from the qualitative interviews, I discuss the limitations of some of these approaches. I conclude by offering some alternatives that,

123

while perhaps not on the radar of most policymakers, would better support all workers in the United States.

CURRENT EMPLOYMENT ADVANCEMENT POLICIES

Various strategies have been suggested by researchers and policy analysts to promote employment advancement among former welfare recipients and low-wage workers. These include using labor market "intermediaries" and other postemployment services to assist low-wage workers in moving into better-paying jobs (Andersson, Holzer, and Lane 2005; Bloom et al. 2005; Holzer and Martinson 2005); increasing opportunities and improving access to educational programs (Strawn and Whistler 2003); and providing financial incentives and raising the minimum wage (Holzer and Martinson 2005).

Labor Market Intermediaries and Postemployment Services

Organizations charged with serving as a conduit between employers and job seekers can be thought of as "labor market intermediaries." These include headhunters and temporary employment agencies, but current and former welfare recipients and low-wage workers are more likely to encounter intermediaries that are the local entities delivering welfare-to-work programs (such as Work First providers) or agencies delivering certain services funded through the Workforce Investment Act (WIA). WIA was designed to be the national system linking business, job seekers, and training providers. One of WIA's mandates was that states create local "one-stop centers," places where those seeking work could get a minimum level of services, including help with their job search and information about job openings.

Harry Holzer and Karin Martinson (2005) note several potential benefits of working with intermediaries. These organizations may be able to provide employers with additional information about job applicants and their skills and thus help overcome potential discrimination against certain types of low-skilled workers. From the applicants' perspective, the intermediary might have information about different firms that could help job seekers make more informed choices. For example, an intermediary might help steer workers away from firms that pay lower-than-average wages or that have a poor track record on promotion and advancement. Information like this might have been useful to Denise, the worker in the family-owned group home who believed she would never advance since she was not related to the owners.

Intermediaries and other social service agencies might also provide support to workers once they are on the job. Services could include referrals to other agencies, career counseling, or case management to help workers manage employment-related problems. A pre-welfare reform evaluation of a national demonstration that provided such assistance found no positive impacts on retention or advancement, although some evidence exists that the programs were not fully implemented (Rangarajan and Novak 1999). The Employment Retention and Advancement (ERA) demonstration, operating after passage of the Personal Responsibility and Work Opportunity Reconciliation Act (PRWORA), similarly found no or very small impacts from the provision of similar types of services (Bloom et al. 2005).

However, the existence of such programs does not mean that their offerings will be utilized. The women we interviewed were very disconnected from the welfare-to-work system, and none seemed to know about services such as those provided through WIA. Only one of the women in the qualitative study had gotten her job through the Work First program; the rest had relied on personal connections and other sources to find jobs. The ERA evaluation has found that engaging people in these services is extremely challenging (Bloom et al. 2005). At one of the sites, some evidence exists that welfare recipients with small monthly grants may have left welfare to avoid participating in the retention and advancement program (Bloom, Hendra, and Page 2006).

Perhaps more challenging is reaching out to low-wage workers who have not been part of the welfare system or for whom participation in welfare occurred long in the past. MDRC, the social science research organization that is leading the evaluation of the retention and advancement initiatives, is also working with two "one-stop" career centers to develop worker advancement programs. These centers have put a great deal of energy into developing marketing strategies to connect to this group of workers and to be distinguished from the welfare and social services systems. Focus groups conducted with low-wage workers indicated that one-stops were not thought of as a place to get help with issues related to advancement and were also viewed negatively by some as being part of the welfare system (Anderson, Kato, and Riccio 2006).

Even if programs can engage participants, any approach that attempts to match workers to higher-paying firms or to counsel job seekers about their career pathways should consider dimensions of a job besides wages and benefits. Quite a few women in the qualitative study were willing to forgo opportunities for higher-paying positions because these upward moves would entail loss of control over schedules because of longer commutes, being on call, or having to work if other employees did not show up for scheduled shifts. Women also made deliberate calculations about whether the potential rise in pay would be more than offset by an unwanted increase in responsibilities. It may be that jobs with higher skills also require women to take on other duties that they do not want.

Education and Training

Increasingly, education matters for getting ahead. According to data from the U.S. Census Bureau, in 2005 adults with a high school diploma could expect to earn just under $30,000. Having an associate's degree increased earnings to just under $38,000, while those with bachelor's degrees averaged more than $54,000. Workers without a high school diploma fared the worst, with expected earnings of just under $20,000 (U.S. Bureau of the Census 2006). Not surprisingly, participating in education and skills programs has been touted as one way for low-wage workers to advance.

Community colleges have traditionally served adults who are returning to school after spending some time in the workforce or who continue to work. Additionally, community colleges are more likely than liberal arts colleges and universities to develop programs and offerings to meet local labor market needs, increasing the likelihood that the skills graduates acquire will lead to jobs (Grubb 2001). However, charting a successful course through the community college or other postsecondary schooling systems poses some challenges.

First, education costs money, in terms of tuition, fees, books, and potentially in lost wages if going to school means cutting back on work hours. Unfortunately, numerous federal and state financial aid packages are not available to students who attend less than half time (Mazzeo et al. 2006), as many of the women we interviewed did. Modifications to financial aid rules, then, might increase access to education for this group of students. In 2006, changes were made to the rules governing administration of the federal Pell Grant program to allow assistance for less than half-time students, a step in the right direction.

Second, over and above financial aid, lower-income students may need support in order to complete an education program. Recall Lorraine, whose prior bad experiences with the educational system, both as a high school student and later in a computer training class, left her confidence shaken. Tia, who was in school when we interviewed her, found it very difficult to juggle her own homework while monitoring her children's, and as a result, her grades suffered. MDRC has begun evaluating different approaches to increase access to education and improve completion rates for lower-income students attending community college. One program operating in Ohio provides intensive, team-based advising to students. Topics are not limited to academic matters; staff members discuss work-family balance and other personal issues. Interviews with students indicated that this service was perceived as extremely valuable to their success (Scrivener and Au 2007). However, the evaluation is not yet far enough along to determine whether this approach will produce positive results on graduation rates.

Participation in education and training activities, and decisions about employment more broadly, may be greatly shaped by women's roles as parents. Many individuals interviewed as part of the qualitative WES were hesitant to take promotions or to return to school for fear of disrupting their children's schedules and/or because of an unwillingness to spend less time with their families. These sentiments were powerful, and the policy solutions discussed thus far could take women who are already working full time out of the home for longer periods of time (e.g., to participate in education and training activities or to take jobs that might demand more time at work). In this case, financial incentives might provide some relief to working families, including those headed by single mothers, in which parents opt to take lower-paying jobs in order to balance family needs.

Financial Incentives and the Minimum Wage

The Earned Income Tax Credit (EITC) has been an important factor in increasing employment and reducing welfare receipt among single mothers (Meyer and Holtz-Eakin 2001). Moreover, it is a major source of support for low-wage working families. Among families with children who received the EITC in 2003, the average credit was $2,100 (Greenstein 2005). However, while the EITC, or other financial strategies such as earned income disregards within the welfare system, may increase employment levels, they may have little effect on advancement. Holzer and Martinson (2005), in their review of the evidence, find that such incentives may increase the amount of time welfare recipients and low-wage workers spend in the labor market. Nevertheless, given the limited returns to experience for this group, more time working will not necessarily lead to increased wages.

On the other hand, additional income in the form of a financial supplement might make women feel that they are being rewarded for their work efforts, as opposed to believing that they are only earning "a few nickels and dimes more." A number of states supplement the federal EITC, but the majority do not. As the Center on Budget and Policy Priorities notes, state EITCs can be quite simple to administer. Most states set their credit as a flat proportion of the federal credit, for example, 30 percent in New York. Furthermore, administrative costs for running a state EITC, assuming they are tied to the federal credit, are modest since monitoring for eligibility of the credit happens at the level of the Internal Revenue Service (see Levitis and Johnson [2006] for more information).

In conjunction with state EITCs, increasing the federal minimum wage could also have a positive effect on low-wage workers. Between 1997 and 2007 the federal minimum wage was $5.15 an hour. While the majority of employees in the WES sample earned above the minimum wage, many were not making much more than this amount. An increase in the wage floor may have the effect of pushing up the pay of all labor near the bottom. Researchers from the Economic Policy Institute call these beneficiaries "indirectly affected workers," arguing that even though employers would not be mandated to raise their wages, empirical evidence suggests that this is what often happens (Economic Policy Institute 2007).[1] As of July 2007, the federal minimum wage rose to

$5.85, with increases to $6.55 set for the following year and $7.25 in 2009.

A strength of state EITCs and minimum wage increases is that they require little to no action on the part of workers. Employees do not have to enroll in any kind of programs or services in order to benefit. Additionally, for women like those in the WES, these policies could be even more beneficial because mothers could take lower-paying jobs that were more conducive to their family lives without suffering such negative financial consequences.

All of the policies described take as a given the current way that work and family life is structured in the United States. Namely, they assume that caregiving responsibilities remain a private matter and that government, to a large extent, should not interfere with what is perceived to be "business practices" (e.g., leave and health care policies). However, perhaps it is time for the United States to consider a new model. Instead of aiming only to support work, as most of the current policies seek to do, the nation could consider doing more to support its workers.

TOWARD A NEW VISION: CHANGING THE WAY WE SUPPORT WORKERS

Many of the challenges faced by working mothers, whether they are the women who participated in the WES or higher-paid executives like those featured in the *New York Times*, are generated by conditions inherent to the way our employment and educational institutions are structured. The Alfred P. Sloan Foundation, a leader in funding research on work and family, states, "While the demographics of the American *workforce* have changed dramatically over the last thirty years, the structure of the American *workplace* has not. It retains its full-time, full-year structure, which no longer makes sense when most employees live in dual-earner or single-parent households [and often have] significant care-giving responsibilities" (Christensen n.d.). For the most part, government does little to regulate leave policies, and firms may have limited incentive to implement more family-friendly approaches, particularly for lower-skilled workers who may be viewed as expendable

(Levin-Epstein 2006). Particularly troubling, health care benefits are tied to employment, and as health care costs continue to rise, employers increasingly are shifting those expenses to employees, who may opt to go without coverage because they cannot afford to insure themselves.

Similarly, our schooling system is based on outdated models that assume 1) children are needed at home during the summer to work on family farms; 2) at least one parent, presumably the mother, will be at home to receive children when they leave school at midafternoon; and 3) postsecondary training will commence upon graduation from high school and will be completed in a continuous fashion. However, possibilities for change do exist.

Workplace Flexibility and Family Leave

First, policies and practices that give workers flexibility to perform caregiving responsibilities need to be viewed as a benefit to business and not just as a perk for employees. These strategies include paid leave and flexible scheduling (e.g., working nonconsecutive hours around appointments or other family obligations, or swapping shifts on short notice). Such approaches can increase worker retention, which can save money, even for firms employing primarily low-wage workers (Levin-Epstein 2006).

The federal government could assume a leadership role in encouraging workplace flexibility. One way would be to mandate some minimum standards around leave beyond those that currently exist (Levin-Epstein 2006). The Family and Medical Leave Act of 1993 guarantees leave for births, adoptions, and medical illnesses, but only employees at larger firms are covered, and the time off is unpaid. However, many of our western European counterparts provide much more much generous leave strategies and could be the model upon which U.S. policy is based. In particular, the Nordic countries of Sweden, Norway, and Finland offer examples of approaches that support parents when they wish to take leave but also make it easier for parents to work while they are raising a family.

These countries are known for their generous policies for new parents: 30–40 weeks of paid leave. Parents in Nordic countries are also entitled to paid time off to take care of ill children. This, too, is a government guarantee, whereas in the United States, such procedures are left to the discretion of employers. These policies typically cover children up to 15 years of age and replace wages at a relatively high level, ranging from about 60 to 70 percent of earnings. Norway allows up to 10 days of leave per child per year, with this time doubled for single parents. While these allowances may strike some in the United States as not feasible because of their potential cost, actual use of leave days is typically much lower than what is legally allowed. For example, Swedish parents use an average of seven days per year of family leave time (Gornick and Meyers 2003).

As noted in Chapter 2, only about half of workers in the WES sample worked in positions offering paid sick days or vacation days, and some lost those benefits when they switched jobs. Making leave time a legal guarantee would put all workers on a par with each other and not make the ability to care for children contingent on the policies of a particular employer.

A Shorter Workweek

A more radical but also necessary move, given changing demographics, would be to shorten the standard workweek. Perhaps a 40-hour workweek made sense when the male-breadwinner/stay-at-home mother was the dominant family form. However, now that dual-earner and single-parent families abound, it is time for the United States to revisit the amount of time we expect individuals to spend at work.

A workweek of under 40 hours would allow parents to devote more time to caregiving responsibilities, something desired by nearly all women in this study. As Janet Gornick and Marcia Meyers (2003), whose book *Families That Work* forms the basis of many of the recommendations in this chapter, note, limiting full-time employment to less than 40 hours a week for all workers increases the likelihood that women would not be penalized. First, in two-parent homes, men may be encouraged to devote more time to family responsibilities, and second, women would not be considered more marginal workers in the way that part-time employees currently are viewed.

Changing Educational Practices

Despite the long hours logged by Americans, the early childhood and secondary school systems of the United States do not match up well to the needs of working parents. Child care for non-school-aged children remains largely a privately funded enterprise. Even though public expenditures for child care increased dramatically after welfare reform, the United States still lags behind other industrialized countries. Despite the availability of public subsidies, an estimated two-thirds of lower-income families with employed mothers, like the women in this study, incur out-of-pocket expenses. This contrasts with only 23 percent of similar families in France (Gornick and Meyers 2003). Greater funding should be set aside for subsidizing high-quality child care for more families.

Typical school schedules do not correspond well with work hours. Although it is likely unwise to extend the school day, particularly for very young children, public funds should be made available for children to participate in activities at recreation centers, perhaps placed at local schools. Both Denmark and Sweden have such policies. The availability of this service would not only ease the minds of working mothers who worry about their children's whereabouts in the after-school hours but could potentially provide lower-income youth with opportunities to participate in extracurricular activities, a task currently made difficult with women's work schedules.

Clearly, many women in our sample wished to pursue additional education for themselves. While the regression analyses did not indicate a relationship between more education and movement into a better-paying job, the larger literature on employment advancement and changes in the U.S. labor market demonstrates a strong link between higher education and higher wages. However, a key challenge for adults, particularly parents, who attend school while working or after being out of a classroom for some time, is being able to finish their degrees (Richburg-Hayes 2008).

Working parents may need to take more time to complete their course of study since they are juggling school with employment and family demands. A move toward a shorter workweek would certainly give some parents more opportunity to devote to educational pursuits. As noted, financial aid packages have typically been structured with the traditional student in mind, one who attends school at least part time and who does not have children to support. Aid packages could be restructured so that they are based upon enrollment in a program (i.e., a course of study leading to a certificate or degree), not the amount of time spent in a program. To encourage persistence toward completion of degrees, federal and state child care funds should be available to lower-wage workers who are in classes (or a class), with allowances for time to study.

Health Care for All

As of 2006, the number of uninsured Americans has risen to 47 million (Center on Budget and Policy Priorities 2007), a figure that includes many of the WES respondents. Expanding access to health care has been a focus of the 2008 presidential campaign. Many others have written extensively about the need for universal health care coverage in the United States, including Angel, Lein, and Henrici (2006). While development of a specific proposal for universal coverage is beyond the scope of this book, some sort of health care mandate is needed.

The women in this study listed health care benefits as a desired attribute of a job. As the cost of private insurance and co-payments rises, it is likely that more and more workers will end up like LaVonda, who chose to forgo her employer's health care coverage because of the expense relative to her wages. The only way out of this dilemma is for the United States to again emulate western European countries and offer all citizens access to basic health care.

Feasibility

None of these policy recommendations come cheaply. However, the cost of such strategies may be more than offset by the benefits they provide. Misra, Moller, and Budig (2007) conducted an analysis of the impact of various work-family policies, finding that state-paid child care is associated with a large reduction in poverty rates. Having fewer families in poverty translates into reduced costs for other social programs, such as food stamps and welfare payments. Further, lack of insurance is a cost not just to the uninsured but to the rest of the nation. Illnesses that could have been averted through preventative care can result in missed days of work and lost productivity. According to a report by the Kaiser Family Foundation, the estimated yearly value of the forgone health of the uninsured exceeds $100 billion, an amount that is more than twice as large as the calculated cost of providing insurance to this group (Hadley and Holahan 2004).

Many other objections to these proposals undoubtedly exist. However, as Gornick and Meyers (2003) note, these policies, in promoting the well-being of families, can be seen as investments in children. If children are public goods, which the authors (and I) argue they are, then the time parents spend providing care in a private setting should be valued to a greater degree. Under our current system, women—in particular, lower-income single mothers—instead incur "costs in the form of employment interruptions, forgone wages, and diminished career opportunities" (Gornick and Meyers 2003, p. 300).

Welfare reform ended the possibility that poor single mothers could receive benefits and stay home and care for their children. Many former welfare recipients are actively engaged in the labor market, some having moved up the employment ladder, but many others still earn relatively low wages. Most women we interviewed believed that their chances to do better were limited because of their responsibilities as parents. When faced with a choice between higher wages or control over their schedules, many chose the latter. As the women we interviewed made clear, their children come first. Policy could do more not only to respect that decision but to help families by better supporting working parents.

Note

1. For a thorough discussion of the multinomial logistic model, see Borooah (2002).

Appendix A
Chapter 3 Regression Results

This appendix includes more information on the variables and models used in the regression analyses reported in Chapter 3.

DESCRIPTIVE RESULTS

The first column of data in Table A.1 displays the overall means and standard deviations for the various measures for the women in the WES sample who started in poverty-wage jobs. The other columns show the means and standard deviations for each transition group: those who stayed in poverty-wage jobs (Group 1), those who moved into above-poverty-wage jobs (Group 2), and those who were later unemployed (Group 3). Table A.2 presents information in the same format for those who started in above-poverty-wage jobs. Superscripts denote significant differences in means across the groups. Please see Table 3.4 in Chapter 3 for a definition of terms.

About 52 percent of women starting in poverty-wage positions were African American and 48 percent were white. Half of the women were between the ages of 25 and 34 in 1997. The majority of sample members, about 73 percent, were never married during the study period. The average number of children residing in the household was about two, and about 20 percent of the sample had at least one additional child come into the house over the study period.

Just over a fifth, 20.7 percent, lacked a high school diploma or GED, although a greater percentage of those who became unemployed, 29.1 percent, lacked this credential, compared to those who moved into higher-paying jobs (15.4 percent). About two-fifths of this sample had obtained education beyond high school by 2003. However, those who had moved into above-poverty-wage jobs (Group 2) were more likely than those in the other groups to have gotten more education (49 percent versus just under a third for both steady poverty-wage workers and the unemployed).

About a tenth of this sample lacked knowledge of appropriate workplace norms, although this number was higher among women starting and staying in poverty-wage jobs, at 13.7 percent. A similar proportion had low levels of work experience, although women who became unemployed were much more likely to have low work experience (24.1 percent). About 16 percent of the sample had not worked in jobs utilizing higher-level skills. About a tenth of the sample

Table A.1 Descriptive Statistics, WES Workers Starting in a Poverty-Wage Job Means and Standard Deviations

	Started in poverty wage $n = 232$	Ended in poverty wage (Group 1) $n = 73$	Ended in above-poverty wage (Group 2) $n = 104$	Ended unemployed (Group 3) $n = 55$
African American	0.522	0.575	0.519	0.455
	(0.501)	(0.498)	(0.502)	(0.503)
White	0.478	0.425	0.481	0.545
	(0.501)	(0.498)	(0.502)	(0.503)
18–24 yrs. old	0.272	0.288	0.279	0.236
	(0.446)	(0.456)	(0.451)	(0.429)
25–34 yrs. old	0.500	0.507	0.490	0.509
	(0.501)	(0.503)	(0.502)	(0.505)
35+ yrs. old	0.228	0.205	0.231	0.255
	(0.421)	(0.407)	(0.423)	(0.440)
Married 0 waves	0.728	0.740	0.750	0.673
	(0.446)	(0.442)	(0.435)	(0.474)
Married 1–2 waves	0.116	0.110	0.125	0.109
	(0.321)	(0.315)	(0.332)	(0.315)
Married 3–5 waves	0.155	0.151	0.125	0.218
	(0.363)	(0.360)	(0.332)	(0.417)
No. of children, 1997	2.194	2.370	2.067	2.200
	(1.231)	(1.328)	(1.126)	(1.282)
No. of children increased	0.207	0.219	0.202	0.200
	(0.406)	(0.417)	(0.403)	(0.404)
No high school/GED	0.207	0.219	0.154	0.291[e]
	(0.406)	(0.417)	(0.363)	(0.458)
High school grad.	0.392	0.452	0.356	0.382
	(0.489)	(0.501)	(0.481)	(0.490)
More than high school	0.401	0.329	0.490[b,f]	0.327
	(0.491)	(0.473)	(0.502)	(0.474)
Work norms barrier	0.099	0.137[c]	0.106	0.036
	(0.299)	(0.346)	(0.309)	(0.189)
Low work exp.	0.104	0.097	0.038	0.241[d,e]
	(0.306)	(0.298)	(0.193)	(0.432)
Low work skills	0.159	0.164	0.144	0.182
	(0.367)	(0.373)	(0.353)	(0.389)

Table A.1 (continued)

	Started in poverty wage $n = 232$	Ended in poverty wage (Group 1) $n = 73$	Ended in above-poverty wage (Group 2) $n = 104$	Ended unemployed (Group 3) $n = 55$
Learning disability	0.099	0.151[a]	0.029	0.164[e]
	(0.299)	(0.360)	(0.168)	(0.373)
Prior discrimination	0.125	0.205[a,c]	0.087	0.091
	(0.331)	(0.407)	(0.283)	(0.290)
No transportation barrier	0.453	0.342	0.548[b]	0.418
	(0.499)	(0.478)	(0.500)	(0.498)
Transp. barrier 1–2 waves	0.267	0.274	0.288	0.218
	(0.443)	(0.449)	(0.455)	(0.417)
Transp. barrier 3–5 waves	0.280	0.384[a]	0.163	0.364[e]
	(0.450)	(0.490)	(0.372)	(0.485)
Mental health prob. 0 waves	0.358	0.342	0.385	0.327
	(0.480)	(0.478)	(0.489)	(0.474)
Mental health prob. 1–2 waves	0.345	0.342[c]	0.423	0.200
	(0.476)	(0.478)	(0.496)	(0.404)
Mental health prob. 3–5 waves	0.297	0.315[a]	0.192	0.473[d,e]
	(0.458)	(0.478)	(0.396)	(0.504)
Physical health prob. 0 waves	0.565	0.575[c]	0.635[f]	0.418
	(0.497)	(0.498)	(0.484)	(0.498)
Physical health prob. 1–2 waves	0.293	0.301	0.288	0.291
	(0.456)	(0.462)	(0.455)	(0.458)
Physical health prob. 3–5 waves	0.142	0.123	0.077	0.291[d,e]
	(0.350)	(0.331)	(0.268)	(0.458)
Child health prob. 0 waves	0.578	0.507	0.625	0.582
	(0.495)	(0.503)	(0.486)	(0.498)
Child health prob. 1–2 waves	0.315	0.411[a,c]	0.288	0.236
	(0.465)	(0.495)	(0.455)	(0.429)
Child health prob. 3–5 waves	0.108	0.082	0.087	0.182[d,e]
	(0.311)	(0.277)	(0.283)	(0.389)
Drug use, 0 waves	0.543	0.425	0.615[b]	0.564
	(0.499)	(0.498)	(0.489)	(0.501)
Drug use, 1–2 waves	0.267	0.329	0.240	0.236
	(0.443)	(0.473)	(0.429)	(0.429)

(continued)

138   Seefeldt

Table A.1 (continued)

	Started in poverty wage $n = 232$	Ended in poverty wage (Group 1) $n = 73$	Ended in above-poverty wage (Group 2) $n = 104$	Ended unemployed (Group 3) $n = 55$
Drug use, 3–5 waves	0.190	0.247[a]	0.144	0.200
	(0.393)	(0.434)	(0.353)	(0.404)
Domestic violence 0 waves	0.599	0.589	0.615	0.582
	(0.491)	(0.495)	(0.489)	(0.498)
Domestic violence 1–2 waves	0.323	0.329	0.327	0.309
	(0.469)	(0.473)	(0.471)	(0.466)
Domestic violence 3–5 waves	0.078	0.082	0.058	0.109
	(0.268)	(0.277)	(0.234)	(0.315)

NOTE: Standard deviations are in parentheses. Significance levels are at least or less than chi-square < 0.10.
[a]Mean for Group 1 significantly greater than for Group 2.
[b]Mean for Group 2 significantly greater than for Group 1.
[c]Mean for Group 1 significantly greater than for Group 3.
[d]Mean for Group 3 significantly greater than for Group 1.
[e]Mean for Group 3 significantly greater than for Group 2.
[f]Mean for Group 2 significantly greater than for Group 3.
SOURCE: Author's tabulations from WES data.

of women starting in poverty-wage jobs had a probable learning disability, but again, this proportion is much higher, 15.1 percent, for those beginning and ending the study period in low-wage jobs and those who became unemployed, 16.4 percent, compared to those who moved up into higher-paying jobs (2.9 percent). Of the women starting in poverty-wage jobs, 12.5 percent reported prior experiences of workplace discrimination, but this figure is higher for the group starting and staying in poverty-wage jobs (20.5 percent, Group 1).

Forty-five percent of those starting in poverty-wage jobs never had a transportation barrier, but this was particularly true for those who had progressed into above-poverty-wage jobs; 54.8 percent of this group never had a transportation barrier. On the other hand, those remaining in poverty-wage jobs and those becoming unemployed were much more likely to have experienced transportation problems in three or more survey waves.

The minority of this sample, 35.8 percent, never experienced a mental health problem during the study. More than a third, 34.5 percent, of those starting in poverty-wage jobs met the diagnostic screening criteria for a mental health problem once or twice during the 1997–2003 period, while another 29.7

Table A.2 Descriptive Statistics, Workers Starting in an Above-Poverty-Wage Job

	Started in above-poverty wage $n = 189$	Ended in poverty wage (Group 1) $n = 39$	Ended in above-poverty wage (Group 2) $n = 110$	Ended unemployed (Group 3) $n = 40$
African American	0.593	0.564	0.636	0.500
	(0.493)	(0.502)	(0.483)	(0.506)
White	0.407	0.436	0.364	0.500
	(0.493)	(0.502)	(0.483)	(0.506)
18–24 yrs. old	0.286	0.282	0.282	0.300
	(0.453)	(0.456)	(0.452)	(0.464)
25–34 yrs. old	0.455	0.410	0.491	0.400
	(0.499)	(0.498)	(0.502)	(0.496)
35+ yrs. old	0.259	0.308	0.227	0.300
	(0.439)	(0.468)	(0.421)	(0.464)
Married 0 waves	0.720	0.795	0.718	0.650
	(0.450)	(0.409)	(0.452)	(0.483)
Married 1–2 waves	0.111	0.077	0.109	0.150
	(0.315)	(0.270)	(0.313)	(0.362)
Married 3–5 waves	0.169	0.128	0.173	0.200
	(0.376)	(0.339)	(0.380)	(0.405)
Number of children, 1997	2.259	2.821[a]	2.045	2.300
	(1.281)	(1.790)	(0.971)	(1.305)
Number of children increased	0.222	0.179	0.236	0.225
	(0.417)	(0.389)	(0.427)	(0.423)
No high school/GED	0.169	0.282[a]	0.118	0.200
	(0.376)	(0.456)	(0.324)	(0.405)
High school grad.	0.354	0.385	0.364	0.300
	(0.480)	(0.493)	(0.483)	(0.464)
More than high school	0.476	0.333	0.518[b]	0.500
	(0.501)	(0.478)	(0.502)	(0.506)
Work norms barrier	0.063	0.051	0.045	0.125[c]
	(0.244)	(0.223)	(0.209)	(0.335)
Low work exp.	0.079	0.026	0.073	0.150[d]
	(0.271)	(0.160)	(0.261)	(0.362)

Table A.2 (continued)

	Started in above-poverty wage $n = 189$	Ended in poverty wage (Group 1) $n = 39$	Ended in above-poverty wage (Group 2) $n = 110$	Ended unemployed (Group 3) $n = 40$
Work skills barrier	0.153	0.154	0.118	0.250[e]
	(0.361)	(0.366)	(0.324)	(0.439)
Learning disability	0.063	0.051	0.036	0.150[e]
	(0.244)	(0.223)	(0.188)	(0.362)
Prior discrimination	0.122	0.051	0.173[b,f]	0.050
	(0.328)	(0.223)	(0.380)	(0.221)
Transp. barrier 0 waves	0.561	0.513	0.618[f]	0.450
	(0.498)	(0.506)	(0.488)	(0.504)
Transp. barrier 1–2 waves	0.249	0.282	0.227	0.275
	(0.433)	(0.456)	(0.421)	(0.452)
Transp. barrier 3–5 waves	0.190	0.205	0.155	0.275[e]
	(0.394)	(0.409)	(0.363)	(0.452)
Mental health prob. 0 waves	0.354	0.333	0.354	0.375
	(0.480)	(0.478)	(0.481)	(0.490)
Mental health prob. 1–2 waves	0.386	0.359	0.391	0.400
	(0.488)	(0.486)	(0.490)	(0.496)
Mental health prob. 3–5 waves	0.259	0.307	0.254	0.225
	(0.439)	(0.467)	(0.437)	(0.423)
Physical health prob. 0 waves	0.561	0.615[e]	0.645[f]	0.275
	(0.498)	(0.493)	(0.481)	(0.452)
Physical health prob. 1–2 waves	0.339	0.205	0.291	0.600[d,e]
	(0.474)	(0.409)	(0.456)	(0.496)
Physical health prob. 3–5 waves	0.101	0.179[a]	0.064	0.125
	(0.302)	(0.389)	(0.245)	(0.335)
Child health prob. 0 waves	0.624	0.538	0.682	0.550
	(0.486)	(0.505)	(0.468)	(0.504)
Child health prob. 1–2 waves	0.291	0.359	0.255	0.325
	(0.455)	(0.486)	(0.438)	(0.474)
Child health prob. 3–5 waves	0.085	0.103	0.064	0.125
	(0.279)	(0.307)	(0.245)	(0.335)
Drug use, 0 waves	0.640	0.615	0.645	0.650
	(0.481)	(0.493)	(0.481)	(0.483)

(continued)

Table A.2 (continued)

	Started in above-poverty wage n = 189	Ended in poverty wage (Group 1) n = 39	Ended in above-poverty wage (Group 2) n = 110	Ended unemployed (Group 3) n = 40
Drug use, 1–2 waves	0.228	0.256	0.236	0.175
	(0.420)	(0.442)	(0.427)	(0.385)
Drug use, 3–5 waves	0.132	0.128	0.118	0.175
	(0.340)	(0.339)	(0.324)	(0.385)
Domestic violence 0 waves	0.651	0.718	0.609	0.700
	(0.478)	(0.456)	(0.490)	(0.464)
Domestic violence 1–2 waves	0.291	0.231	0.318	0.275
	(0.455)	(0.427)	(0.468)	(0.452)
Domestic violence 3–5 waves	0.058	0.051	0.073	0.025
	(0.235)	(0.223)	(0.261)	(0.158)

NOTE: Standard deviations are in parentheses. Significance levels are at least or less than chi-square < 0.10.
[a]Mean for Group 1 significantly greater than for Group 2.
[b]Mean for Group 2 significantly greater than for Group 1.
[c]Mean for Group 1 significantly greater than for Group 3.
[d]Mean for Group 3 significantly greater than for Group 1.
[e]Mean for Group 3 significantly greater than for Group 2.
[f]Mean for Group 2 significantly greater than for Group 3.
SOURCE: Author's tabulations from WES data.

percent had what could be termed persistent mental health problems, experiencing some difficulty in at least three survey waves. Women who moved into above-poverty-wage jobs were less likely (19.2 percent) than the other two groups (31.5 of those ending in poverty-wage jobs and 47.3 percent of those who became unemployed) to have had mental health problems in three to five survey waves, and those ending the period in poverty-wage jobs were more likely than the unemployed to have mental health problems in one or two waves. The majority of this sample, 56.5 percent, did not experience a physical health problem during the study, but those who remained employed were more likely, relative to the unemployed, to never have had a health problem. Conversely, those who became unemployed by 2003 (Group 3) were more likely (29.1 percent) than the other two groups to have had persistent physical health problems. While the majority of this sample never reported that any children had health-related problems, women who maintained poverty-wage employment were more likely than those who moved up or those who became unemployed to have a child with health problems in one or two survey waves. On the other hand, women who became unemployed were more than twice as likely (18.2 percent versus about 8 percent) as those in the other two groups to report children with persistent health problems.

More than half of all women who started off in poverty-wage jobs reported that they never used illicit drugs during the study, and this is particularly true for those who advanced (61.5 percent). Just under a fifth of this sample reported drug use in three or more waves, and those remaining in poverty-wage jobs were more likely to report chronic drug use (24.7 percent) than those who moved into above-poverty-wage jobs (14.4 percent). A majority of respondents, 59.9 percent, never experienced domestic violence, about a third experienced partner violence in one or two survey waves, and 7.8 percent experienced persistent abuse. No significant differences exist between the groups on this barrier.

Table A.2 shows the same information for the sample of workers who started in above-poverty-wage jobs in 1997/1998. Again, the first column shows the descriptive statistics for this entire sample, while the subsequent columns report on those who ended the study period in poverty-wage jobs (Group 1), in above-poverty-wage jobs (Group 2), or unemployed (Group 3). This sample was about 60 percent African American and 40 percent white, and just under half of the women were between the ages of 25 and 34 in 1997. This is also a sample that was predominantly never married during WES data collection (72 percent). Compared to women starting in poverty-wage jobs (Table A.1), the number of children living in households of women starting in above-poverty-wage jobs in 1997 is slightly larger at about 2.3 children. In part, this is because women who experienced downward employment movement (Group 1) were more likely to have larger family sizes (closer to three than two children) than those who maintained above-poverty-wage employment. About one-fifth of these women had additional children over the course of the study.

Just under 17 percent of this sample lacked a high school diploma or GED by study's end, although this proportion is higher for women with downward employment transitions (28.2 percent, Group 1) compared to those who maintained above-poverty-wage employment (11.8 percent, Group 2). Conversely, women who remained in above-poverty-wage jobs were more likely to have additional years of education beyond high school in 2003, compared to the group who moved down the employment ladder (51.8 versus 33.3 percent).

In terms of other human capital characteristics, just over 6 percent of the sample of those starting in above-poverty-wage jobs lacked knowledge of appropriate workplace norms, although significant differences exist between those who ended unemployed (12.5 percent) and those who remained in above-poverty-wage jobs (4.5 percent). A slightly higher proportion, just under 8 percent, had low prior work experience, with those who became unemployed being significantly more likely to have this barrier compared to those who had downward employment transitions (15 percent for Group 3 versus 2.6 percent for Group 1). About 15 percent had worked only in jobs using few higher-level skills. Again, those who became unemployed were much more likely to have this barrier (25 percent of this group) compared to those remaining in above-poverty-wage jobs (11.8 percent). About 6 percent of those starting out in above-poverty-wage jobs had likely learning disabilities, with higher rates (15 percent) among the unemployed than among those remaining in above-poverty-wage jobs (just 3.6 percent). About 12 percent reported prior experiences of workplace discrimination. On this measure, those remaining in above-poverty-wage jobs were more likely than the other two groups to report discrimination (17.3 percent versus about 5 percent).

The slight majority of the sample of women starting in above-poverty-wage jobs never had a transportation barrier as I defined it, although workers who were able to maintain above-poverty-wage jobs (Group 2) were more likely than those who became unemployed (Group 3) to never have had this problem (61.8 percent versus 45 percent). The unemployed, though, were more likely than steady above-poverty-wage workers to have persistent transportation problems throughout the period, with 27.5 percent of those who moved from an above-poverty-wage job to unemployment reporting that they lacked a car and/or driver's license at three or more survey waves.

Mental health problems were not uncommon; only 35.4 percent of this sample never met the diagnostic screening criteria for any mental health disorder. Physical health problems were slightly less common, but just over a third of the sample reported a physical health limitation and fair/poor health one or two times, and another tenth had persistent physical health problems. Those who became unemployed were much more likely to have physical health problems in one to two survey waves, while those who moved from above-poverty-wage jobs to poverty-wage work were more likely than those remaining in above-poverty-wage jobs to report physical health problems three or more times. About 6 in 10 women never reported having children with health limitations.

Reported drug use was less among those starting in above-poverty-wage jobs (64 percent never used) than among those starting in poverty-wage jobs (54.3 percent never used, Table A.1). Finally, about two-thirds of the sample of women starting in above-poverty-wage jobs never experienced domestic violence during the study, with no significant differences between groups.

MULTIVARIATE ANALYSES

The results reported in Chapter 3 come from a series of multinomial logistic regressions that compute the likelihood of being in one of the various employment transition groups, relative to another.[1] These regressions were run separately for those starting in poverty-wage jobs and those starting in above-poverty-wage jobs. In this series of regressions, the comparison groups are those who later became employed, although post-hoc analyses were conducted using the Wald test to determine whether significant differences existed between the coefficients for the result of remaining in the starting category, relative to moving to the other employed category.

Logistic regression applies maximum likelihood estimation after transforming the dependent variable (in this case, the employment transition groups) into the natural log of the odds of the dependent variable occurring or not. In simple terms, it estimates the probability of the occurrence of an event (Garson 2006). However, since the coefficient calculates changes in the natural log of the odds of the dependent variable, interpretation is not as straightforward as ordinary least squares (OLS) regression. For ease, I will refer to coefficients with positive values as "increasing the natural log of the odds" and those with negative values as "decreasing the natural log of the odds."

Tables A.3 and A.4 show the coefficients and standard errors for the different variables. Table A.3 presents the results for those starting in poverty-wage jobs, and Table A.4 presents results for those starting in above-poverty-wage jobs. The top halves of both tables show the results for those ending the study period in poverty-wage jobs; the bottom halves of the tables show results for those ending in above-poverty-wage jobs, with all results relative to becoming unemployed by 2003. Since most of the variables in these regressions are dummy variables, the results are also relative to the omitted category for that variable.

For example, the coefficient on the work norms variable in the top half of Table A.3 would be interpreted as follows: having the work norms barrier in 1997, *relative to not having it*, is associated with an increase in the natural log of the odds of remaining in a poverty-wage job, relative to becoming unemployed. The significance of the work experience variable can be interpreted as the following: having low work experience in 1997, *relative to not having this barrier*, is associated with a significant decrease in the natural log of the odds of staying in a poverty-wage job, *relative to becoming unemployed* and relative to moving into an above-poverty-wage job (see both halves of the table). The interpretation of all results is discussed in Chapter 3.

Table A.3 Multinomial Regression Results for WES Workers, for Those Starting in Poverty-Wage Jobs, Relative to Those Ending Unemployed (*n* = 229)

| | End in poverty-wage job | | | |
Variable	Coefficient	Standard error	Z score	P > |z|
African American	−0.1632	0.4697	−0.350	0.728
Age 25–34	−0.3016	0.5460	−0.550	0.581
Age 35+	−0.3551	0.6789	−0.520	0.601
Married 1–2 waves	−0.1789	0.6867	−0.260	0.794
Married 3–5 waves	−0.5023	0.6221	−0.810	0.419
Number of children, 1997	0.1751	0.1955	0.900	0.371
Number of children increased	−0.4227	0.5468	−0.770	0.440
No high school/GED	−0.4382	0.6053	−0.720	0.469
More than high school	−0.3849	0.5020	−0.770	0.443
Work norms barrier	1.4754	0.8699	1.700	0.090*
Low work experience	−1.5858	0.6712	−2.360	0.018**
Work skills barrier	0.5981	0.6638	0.900	0.368
Learning disability	0.4944	0.7105	0.700	0.487
Prior discrimination	2.0391	0.7727	2.640	0.008***
Transportation barrier 1–2 waves	0.4159	0.5563	0.750	0.455
Transportation barrier 3–5 waves	0.5937	0.6042	0.980	0.326
Mental health problem 1–2 waves	0.7933	0.5754	1.380	0.168
Mental health problem 3–5 waves	−0.0420	0.5736	−0.070	0.942
Physical health problem 1–2 waves	−0.7903	0.5136	−1.540	0.124
Physical health problem 3–5 waves	−1.4270	0.7000	−2.040	0.041**
Child health problem 1–2 waves	0.6750	0.4972	1.360	0.175
Child health problem 3–5 waves	−0.5383	0.7819	−0.690	0.491
Drug use 1–2 waves	0.6078	0.5439	1.120	0.264
Drug use 3–5 waves	0.2295	0.5858	0.390	0.695
Domestic violence 1–2 waves	−0.2658	0.5146	−0.520	0.606
Domestic violence 3–5 waves	0.2208	0.8687	0.250	0.799
Constant	0.0620	0.8070	0.080	0.939

(continued)

Table A.3 (continued)

	End in above-poverty-wage job			
Variable	Coefficient	Standard error	Z score	$P > \|z\|$
African American	0.0671	0.4407	0.150	0.879
Age 25–34	−0.1151	0.5162	−0.220	0.824
Age 35+	0.4662	0.6425	0.730	0.468
Married 1–2 waves	−0.0635	0.6570	−0.100	0.923
Married 3–5 waves	−0.7194	0.5905	−1.220	0.223
Number of children, 1997	−0.1610	0.1892	−0.850	0.395
Number of children increased	−0.3009	0.5235	−0.570	0.565
No high school/GED	0.2637	0.6099	0.430	0.666
More than high school	0.2425	0.4719	0.510	0.607
Work norms barrier	1.0327	0.8710	1.190	0.236
Low work experience	−2.5149	0.7505	−3.350	0.001***
Work skills barrier	1.1652	0.6617	1.760	0.078*
Learning disability	−0.7829	0.8822	−0.890	0.375
Prior discrimination	0.9122	0.8098	1.130	0.260
Transportation barrier 1–2 waves	0.2498	0.5144	0.490	0.627
Transportation barrier 3–5 waves	−1.0372	0.5884	−1.760	0.078*
Mental health problem 1–2 waves	1.0169	0.5438	1.870	0.061*
Mental health problem 3–5 waves	−0.4397	0.5514	−0.800	0.425
Physical health problem 1–2 waves	−0.3389	0.4883	−0.690	0.488
Physical health problem 3–5 waves	−1.6445	0.6970	−2.360	0.018**
Child health problem 1–2 waves	0.2553	0.4847	0.530	0.598
Child health problem 3–5 waves	−0.1657	0.7330	−0.230	0.821
Drug use, 1–2 waves	0.1860	0.5276	0.350	0.724
Drug use, 3–5 waves	−0.4473	0.5704	−0.780	0.433
Domestic violence, 1–2 waves	0.4642	0.4789	0.970	0.332
Domestic violence, 3–5 waves	0.7497	0.8833	0.850	0.396
Constant	1.1456	0.7485	1.530	0.126

NOTE: The last column of the table is the p-value or the probability that the coefficient is statistically significant from zero. * = $z < 0.10$; ** = $z < 0.05$; *** = $z < 0.01$.
SOURCE: Author's tabulations from WES data.

Table A.4 Multinomial Regression Results for Those Starting in Above-Poverty-Wage Jobs, Relative to Those Ending Unemployed (*n* = 189)

	End in poverty-wage job			
Variable	Coefficient	Standard error	Z score	P > |z|
African American	0.5133	0.7271	0.710	0.480
Age 25–34	−0.4059	0.7694	−0.530	0.598
Age 35+	−0.1701	0.8561	−0.200	0.843
Married 1–2 waves	−0.6900	1.0045	−0.690	0.492
Married 3–5 waves	−2.2042	0.9053	−2.430	0.015**
Number of children, 1997	0.4871	0.2587	1.880	0.060*
Number of children increased	−0.0040	0.7870	−0.010	0.996
No high school/GED	1.6620	0.9109	1.820	0.068*
More than high school	−1.2783	0.6979	−1.830	0.067*
Work norms barrier	−1.2742	1.3065	−0.980	0.329
Low work experience	−3.8564	1.6616	−2.320	0.020**
Work skills barrier	−0.3803	0.8011	−0.470	0.635
Learning disability	−1.8018	1.1587	−1.560	0.120
Prior discrimination	−0.1034	1.1699	−0.090	0.930
Transp. barrier 1–2 waves	−0.5690	0.7860	−0.720	0.469
Transp. barrier 3–5 waves	−1.4566	0.9823	−1.480	0.138
Mental health problem 1–2 waves	0.1358	0.7214	0.190	0.851
Mental health problem 3–5 waves	0.9762	0.8205	1.190	0.234
Physical health problem 1–2 waves	−2.8436	0.7262	−3.920	0.000***
Physical health problem 3–5 waves	−0.0026	0.9421	0.000	0.998
Child health problem 1–2 waves	0.6124	0.6881	0.890	0.373
Child health problem 3–5 waves	−0.0631	1.0467	−0.060	0.952
Drug use, 1–2 waves	0.6937	0.7444	0.930	0.351
Drug use, 3–5 waves	−0.7233	0.9120	−0.790	0.428
Domestic violence 1–2 waves	−0.0959	0.7534	−0.130	0.899
Domestic violence 3–5 waves	2.0926	1.5456	1.350	0.176
Constant	0.9593	1.1151	0.860	0.390

(continued)

Table A.4 (continued)

	End in above-poverty-wage job			
Variable	Coefficient	Standard error	Z score	P > |z|
African American	0.9821	0.5789	1.700	0.090*
Age 25–34	0.4183	0.6139	0.680	0.496
Age 35+	−0.0669	0.7121	−0.090	0.925
Married 1–2 waves	−0.8622	0.7964	−1.080	0.279
Married 3–5 waves	−1.1646	0.6489	−1.790	0.073*
Number of children, 1997	−0.1595	0.2244	−0.710	0.477
Number of children increased	−0.1839	0.6212	−0.300	0.767
No high school/GED	−0.1224	0.7831	−0.160	0.876
More than high school	−0.8315	0.5690	−1.460	0.144
Work norms barrier	−1.6781	0.9432	−1.780	0.075*
Low work experience	−0.5503	0.8449	−0.650	0.515
Work skills barrier	−0.4622	0.6406	−0.720	0.471
Learning disability	−1.3580	0.8382	−1.620	0.105
Prior discrimination	1.1290	0.8841	1.280	0.202
Transp. barrier 1–2 waves	−0.9144	0.6444	−1.420	0.156
Transp. barrier 3–5 waves	−1.8563	0.8200	−2.260	0.024**
Mental health problem 1–2 waves	0.0996	0.5585	0.180	0.859
Mental health problem 3–5 waves	0.4336	0.6855	0.630	0.527
Physical health problem 1–2 waves	−1.7776	0.5424	−3.280	0.001***
Physical health problem 3–5 waves	−1.1630	0.8230	−1.410	0.158
Child health problem 1–2 waves	0.3266	0.5603	0.580	0.560
Child health problem 3–5 waves	−0.3729	0.8567	−0.440	0.663
Drug use, 1–2 waves	0.4747	0.6156	0.770	0.441
Drug use, 3–5 waves	−1.0022	0.7459	−1.340	0.179
Domestic violence 1–2 waves	0.8644	0.5911	1.460	0.144
Domestic violence 3–5 waves	2.7601	1.3695	2.020	0.044*
Constant	2.7783	0.9692	2.870	0.004

NOTE: The last column of the table is the *p*-value or the probability that the coefficient is statistically significant from zero. * = $z < 0.10$; ** = $z < 0.05$; *** = $z < 0.01$.
SOURCE: Author's tabulations from WES data.

Appendix B
Qualitative Data Methods

This appendix provides more information for the reader interested in the methods used to draw the qualitative sample from the larger WES survey sample. Conducting a qualitative study embedded within an existing panel survey afforded me a unique opportunity to select a set of women to interview based upon the issues of interest to me. I also provide details on the interviewing methods and the process used to code and analyze the data.

SAMPLE SELECTION

Because of my interest in issues related to employment advancement and the challenges of work-family balance, I limited the qualitative sample to women who had fairly steady employment records (and thus had some chance of progression) and to women who still had minor-aged children living in the household. I defined steady employment as having worked in at least 75 percent of the 55 months between the wave 1 and wave 4 surveys. I also decided to limit the sample to women who had at least one resident child aged 14 or younger at the wave 4 (2001) survey. By the time the wave 5 interview was conducted in 2003, this would mean that women would have had at least one child aged 16 or younger, and the likelihood that this child lived with her was still high.[1] Further, because I wanted to make use of all five waves of survey data and because of potential difficulties in locating respondents who had not participated in the fifth survey wave, I also put in as a selection criterion being in the full panel of the WES.[2] I determined that the qualitative sample members should be employed at the time that they were surveyed for the fourth and fifth waves (although as we will see, this did not ensure that they were employed when we interviewed them for the qualitative supplement).

The latter criterion, participation in all five survey waves, is not necessarily a restriction, considering that the multivariate analyses only use cases with valid data for all five survey waves. However, the other restrictions put in place did exclude certain respondents from being in the qualitative sample. Assuming that 536, the number of women who completed the wave 5 survey, is the starting point, each criterion I imposed excluded women from potentially being in the qualitative sample. The first cut I made was to eliminate women who had not worked in at least 75 percent of the months. This standard resulted in losing 270 of the 536 cases, leaving 266 cases that might be eligible for the supplement. Next dropped were those who were not employed at the wave 4 and 5 interviews. This restriction had the effect of eliminating another 39 cases. Finally, 43 additional cases were excluded because no minor-aged children lived in the house. In total, 184 of the 536 WES wave 5 respondents, a little more than one-third, were eligible for the qualitative study.

The selection criteria for the qualitative sample make clear that the women interviewed for this portion of the study are not necessarily representative of the larger WES survey sample. The larger WES survey sample was designed to be a random sample representing the universe of cash assistance recipients in the one urban Michigan county in which these women resided in the month of February 1997. However, the conventions used to determine samples for large-scale surveys and those used in qualitative research are not always the same. In designing the qualitative sample, I followed an approach known as "purposeful sampling" (Marshall 1996). That is, I chose a sample containing people who would most likely be able to help me answer my research questions. Since I was interested in why some women were able to advance further than others, despite steady work, I wanted a sample of women with fairly regular employment records. Additionally, because I was interested in exploring work-family balance issues within the context of the low-wage labor market, I chose to interview only women with children still living at home.

The next step was to draw the interview sample from these 184 cases. To do this, cases were stratified by race and by wage rate, so as to achieve a racial composition similar to that of the overall sample (approximately 45 percent white and 55 percent African American) and a wage distribution reflecting that of employed sample members (about 42 percent in jobs paying more than $9 an hour and the balance in lower-paying jobs). A random number generator was used to choose 30 cases for these interviews. For purposes of comparison, I supplemented these cases with another five individuals who, while employed at the wave 5 interview, with fairly steady work records, did not have a high school diploma or GED at the time of the wave 1 interview (women meeting the initial eligibility criterion for the employment segment were significantly more likely to have a high school diploma or equivalent when they were first surveyed). Again, using a random number generator, I selected three African American and two white cases, with variation in wage rates and with several who were employed in slightly under 75 percent of the study months.

Of the 35 women selected, 32, or 91 percent, were successfully located and interviewed.[3] Despite the limitations we placed upon our qualitative sample, the women closely resembled the rest of the sample in many ways. Table B.1 compares the qualitative sample members to the remaining WES wave 5 respondents on the measures used in the regression analyses presented in Chapter 3.

Table B.1 Demographic, Human Capital, and Employment Barriers, Qualitative and Rest of WES Sample

Characteristic	Qualitative sample (%) ($n = 32$)	Rest of WES sample (%) ($n = 504$)
African American	56.3	54.6
White	43.8	45.4
Age 18–24	25.0	25.0
Age 25–34	53.1	47.8
Age 35+	21.9	27.2
Never married	87.5	71.6*
Married 1–2 waves	6.3	11.3
Married 3–5 waves	6.3	17.1
Number of children, 1997	2.4	2.2
Number of children increased	12.5	22.0
No high school/GED	15.6	23.4
High school graduate	53.1	36.5*
More than high school	31.3	40.1
Learning disability	15.6	13.1
Low work experience	6.3	14.4
Work skills barrier	6.3	22.0**
Work norms barrier	9.4	8.5
Perceived discrimination	12.5	14.9
Never any transportation problem	53.1	45.6
Transportation problem 1–2 waves	34.4	25.6
Transportation problem 3+ waves	12.5	28.8**
No mental health problem	34.4	31.6
Mental health problem 1–2 waves	34.4	37.9
Mental health problem 3+ waves	31.3	30.6
No physical health problem	59.4	50.6
Physical health problem 1–2 waves	31.3	31.0
Physical health problem 3–5 waves	9.4	18.5
Never child with health problem	56.3	57.7
Child with health problem 1–2 waves	34.4	30.0
Child with health problem 3–5 waves	9.4	12.3
No drug use	56.3	58.5
Drug use 1–2 waves	25.0	24.4
Drug use 3–5 waves	18.6	17.1
No domestic violence	78.1	62.1*
Domestic violence 1–2 waves	15.6	30.0*
Domestic violence 3–5 waves	6.3	7.9

NOTE: * difference significant at $p < 0.10$, ** difference significant at $p < 0.05$.
SOURCE: Author's tabulations from WES data.

As seen in Table B.1, the qualitative sample is similar to the rest of the WES sample on most demographic measures. Approximately the same proportions fall into the various age ranges, and the two groups had the same number of children at the baseline. While rates of marriage were not statistically different between qualitative sample members and other WES respondents, the qualitative sample was more likely never to have been married during the years of the WES, compared to the rest of the sample (87.5 percent versus 71.6 percent). More women in the balance of the WES sample saw the number of children in the household increase during the course of the study (22 percent), compared to the qualitative sample (12.5 percent), but this result is not statistically significant.

On most baseline measures of human capital, qualitative sample members also are similar to the larger WES survey sample, although a few differences are present. Qualitative sample members were much less likely to have worked in jobs where they utilized few skills: 6.3 percent of the qualitative sample had the low-skills barrier compared to 22 percent of the rest of the sample.

In terms of the impediments that were measured over time, qualitative sample members were less likely to have very persistent transportation problems (12.5 percent versus 28.8 percent). Additionally, women in the qualitative sample were less likely to have experienced domestic violence. Just under four-fifths of qualitative sample members (78.1 percent) never reported severe partner abuse, while this was true for three-fifths of the rest of the sample. Qualitative sample members were also half as likely to report domestic violence in one or two survey waves (15.6 percent versus 30 percent).

INTERVIEW METHODS

Although women in the qualitative sample had completed the fifth WES survey about three to six months prior to the start of the qualitative part of the study, we recontacted them to solicit their participation. All women were first sent a letter, informing them of the additional interview and the ways in which it differed from the survey. Potential respondents were informed that this interview would give them the opportunity to talk in more detail about some of the issues raised in the various surveys. Next, a member of the interview team, which included the author and three other graduate-level researchers, contacted the respondent, typically by phone although occasionally in person, to set up a time to conduct the interview. In most cases, this process was fairly quick. However, repeated attempts were needed to locate some women, particularly because a number of them had moved. Respondents were paid $30 for their participation.

The interviews were tape-recorded and subsequently transcribed into word processing documents. These documents were imported into a qualitative data analysis software, *Atlas.ti,* which allowed two research assistants and me to read through the transcripts systematically to code and analyze them. For example, for certain topics, we read text segments associated with questions that were asked directly in the interviews (e.g., "What are the characteristics of a good job?"). We also read and reread the entirety of the interviews, more than 1,100 pages of text in total, to determine whether responses given to other interview questions were related to our various topics of interest. In all cases, we developed lists of recurring answers or "themes" and were able to quantify some of the more common ideas. This was an iterative process, with additional coding schemes emerging as we read through the transcripts. In order to assure external validity, we separately read and coded parts of the interviews, comparing results and resolving any inconsistencies in the coding. I also wrote detailed memos about each of the women in the study, which, in addition to synthesizing their demographic and employment experiences in one place, highlighted interesting things they had to say about work, family, and getting ahead.

Notes

1. We were developing the WES qualitative sampling criteria during the final months of data collection for the wave 5 interview.
2. As noted in earlier chapters, the WES experienced attrition, although in a random manner (Cadena and Pape 2006). However, once a woman left the sample, she was not recontacted to participate in future survey waves. For example, if a respondent who had participated in the first and second survey waves (1997 and 1998) could not be located for the third wave in 1999, she was not recontacted for subsequent survey waves.
3. Of the three women from the original qualitative sample who were not interviewed, two could not be contacted despite dozens of phone calls, repeated mailings of letters, and several visits to their homes in an attempt to find them in person. The third declined to participate since she had recently lost her home to a fire and was attempting to find new housing and cope with this traumatic situation.

References

Acs, Gregory, and Pamela Loprest. 2004. *Leaving Welfare: Employment and Well-Being of Families That Left Welfare in the Post-Entitlement Era.* Kalamazoo, MI: W.E. Upjohn Institute for Employment Research.

Adams, Gina, and Monica Rohacek. 2002. "More than a Work Support? Issues around Integrating Child Development Goals into the Child Care Subsidy System." *Early Childhood Research Quarterly* 17: 418–440.

Anderson, Jacquelyn, Linda Yuriko Kato, and James Riccio. 2006. "A New Approach to Low-Wage Workers and Employers." Report to the funders of the Launching the Work Advancement and Support Center Demonstration. New York: MDRC.

Anderson, Jacquelyn, and Karin Martinson. 2003. "Service Delivery and Institutional Linkages: Early Implementation Experiences of Employment Retention and Advancement Programs." Report to the Administration for Children and Families, U.S. Department of Health and Human Services. New York: MDRC.

Andersson, Fredrik, Harry J. Holzer, and Julia Lane. 2005. *Moving Up or Moving On: Who Advances in the Low-Wage Labor Market?* New York: Russell Sage Foundation.

Angel, Ronald J., Laura Lein, and Jane Henrici. 2006. *Poor Families in America's Health Care Crisis.* New York: Cambridge University Press.

Arias, Elizabeth. 2007. *United States Life Tables, 2004.* National Vital Statistics Report 56(9). Hyattsville, MD: National Center for Health Statistics.

Autor, David H., and Susan N. Houseman. 2005. "Do Temporary Help Jobs Improve Labor Market Outcomes for Low-Skilled Workers? Evidence from Random Assignments." W.E. Upjohn Institute Working Paper no. 05-124. Kalamazoo, MI: W.E. Upjohn Institute for Employment Research. http://www.upjohninstitute.org/publications/wp/05-124.pdf (accessed October 9, 2008).

Berg, Linnea, Lynn Olsen, and Aimee Conrad. 1991. "Causes and Implications of Rapid Job Loss among Participants in a Welfare-to-Work Program." Working Paper. Evanston, IL: Center for Urban Affairs and Policy Research.

Bernhardt, Annette D., Martina Morris, Mark S. Handcock, and Marc A. Scott. 2001. *Divergent Paths: Economic Mobility in the New American Labor Market.* New York: Russell Sage Foundation.

Bernstein, Jared, Chauna Brocht, and Maggie Spade-Aguilar. 2000. *How Much Is Enough? Basic Family Budgets for Working Families.* Washington, DC: Economic Policy Institute.

Bloom, Dan, Mary Ferrell, and Barbara Fink. 2002. "Welfare Time Limits: State Policies, Implementation, and Effects on Families." Report to the U.S. Department of Health and Human Services. New York: MDRC.

Bloom, Dan, Richard Hendra, Karin Martinson, and Susan Scrivener. 2005. "The Employment Retention and Advancement Project: Early Results from Four Sites." Report to the U.S. Department of Health and Human Services. New York: MDRC.

Bloom, Dan, Richard Hendra, and Jocelyn Page. 2006. "The Employment Retention and Advancement Project: Results from the Chicago ERA Site." Report to the U.S. Department of Health and Human Services. New York: MDRC.

Bobo, Lawrence D., and Susan A. Suh. 2000. "Surveying Racial Discrimination: Analyses from a Multiethnic Labor Market." In *Prismatic Metropolis: Inequality in Los Angeles*, M. Oliver, L. Bobo, J. Johnson, Jr., and A. Valenzuela, Jr., eds. New York: Russell Sage Foundation, pp. 523–560.

Borooah, Vani Kant. 2002. *Logit and Probit: Ordered and Multinomial Models*. Thousand Oaks, CA: Sage Publications, Inc.

Bureau of Labor Statistics. 2007. "Occupational Outlook Handbook, 2008–09 Edition." Washington, DC: U.S. Department of Labor. http://www.bls.gov/oco/home.htm (accessed July 2008).

Cadena, Brian, and Andreas Pape. 2006. "The Extent and Consequences of Attrition in the Women's Employment Study." Program on Poverty and Social Welfare Policy Working Paper. Ann Arbor, MI: University of Michigan. http://www.fordschool.umich.edu/research/poverty/pdf/WES_attrition_06.pdf (accessed October 9, 2008).

Center on Budget and Policy Priorities. 2007. "The Number of Uninsured Americans Is at an All-Time High." Washington, DC: Center on Budget and Policy Priorities. http://www.cbpp.org/8-29-06health.htm (accessed August 20, 2008).

Christensen, Kathleen. n.d. "History of the Workplace, Work Force and Working Families Program." New York: Alfred P. Sloan Foundation. http://www.sloan.org/programs/Working_Families_History.shtml (accessed August 20, 2008).

Corcoran, Mary, Sandra K. Danziger, and Richard Tolman. 2004. "Long Term Employment of African-American and White Welfare Recipients and the Role of Persistent Health and Mental Health Problems." *Women & Health* 39(4): 21–40.

Danziger, Sandra K., Mary Corcoran, Sheldon Danziger, Colleen Heflin, Ariel Kalil, Judith Levine, Daniel Rosen, Kristin Seefeldt, Kristine Siefert, and Richard Tolman. 2000. "Barriers to the Employment of Welfare Recipients." In *Prosperity for All? The Economic Boom and African Americans*,

R. Cherry and W. M. Rodgers, eds. New York: Russell Sage Foundation, pp. 245–278.

Danziger, Sheldon, and Peter Gottschalk. 1995. *America Unequal.* New York: Russell Sage Foundation.

Danziger, Sheldon, Colleen M. Heflin, Mary E. Corcoran, Elizabeth Oltmans, and Hui-Chen Wang. 2002. "Does It Pay to Move from Welfare to Work?" *Journal of Policy Analysis and Management* 21(4): 671–692.

Economic Policy Institute. 2001. "Living Wage: Facts at a Glance." Washington, DC: Economic Policy Institute. http://www.epi.org/content.cfm /issueguides_livingwage_livingwagefacts (accessed October 9, 2008).

———. 2006. "EPI Issue Guide: Living Wage." Washington, DC: Economic Policy Institute. http://www.epi.org/content.cfm/issueguides_livingwage_ livingwage (accessed October 9, 2008).

———. 2007. "EPI Issue Guide: Minimum Wage." Washington, DC: Economic Policy Institute. http://www.epi.org/content.cfm/issueguides_ minwage (accessed October 9, 2008).

Edin, Kathryn, and Maria Kefalas. 2005. *Promises I Can Keep: Why Poor Women Put Motherhood Before Marriage.* Berkeley, CA: University of California Press.

Edin, Kathryn, and Laura Lein. 1997. *Making Ends Meet: How Single Mothers Survive Welfare and Low-Wage Work.* New York: Russell Sage Foundation.

Ehrenreich, Barbara. 2001. *Nickel and Dimed: On (Not) Getting By in America.* New York: Metropolitan Books.

Erickcek, George A., Susan Houseman, and Arne Kalleberg. 2002. "The Effects of Temporary Services and Contracting Out on Low-Skilled Workers: Evidence from Auto Suppliers, Hospitals, and Public Schools." W.E. Upjohn Institute Working Paper no. 03–90. Kalamazoo, MI: W.E. Upjohn Institute for Employment Research. http://www.upjohninstitute.org/publications/ wp/03-90.pdf (accessed October 9, 2008).

Fuller, Bruce, Sharon L. Kagan, Gretchen L. Caspary, and Christiane A. Gauthier. 2002. "Welfare Reform and Child Care Options for Low-Income Families." *The Future of Children* 12(1): 97–120.

Garson, G. David. 2006. "Logistic Regression." In *Statnotes: Topics in Multivariate Analysis.* http://faculty.chass.ncsu.edu/garson/pa765/logistic.htm (accessed October 9, 2008).

Goldin, Claudia. 2006. "Working It Out." *New York Times*, March 15, A:27.

Gornick, Janet, and Marcia K. Meyers. 2003. *Families That Work: Policies for Reconciling Parenthood and Employment.* New York: Russell Sage Foundation.

Greenstein, Robert. 2005. "The Earned Income Tax Credit: Boosting Employment, Aiding the Working Poor." Washington, DC: Center on Budget and Policy Priorities.

Grubb, W. Norton. 2001. "Second Chances in Changing Times: The Roles of Community Colleges in Advancing Low-Skilled Workers." In *Low-Wage Workers in the New Economy: Strategies for Opportunity and Advancement*, Richard Kazis and Marc Miller, eds. Washington, DC: Urban Institute, pp 283–306.

Hadley, Jack, and John Holahan. 2004. "The Cost of Care for the Uninsured: What Do We Spend, Who Pays, and What Would Full Coverage Add to Medical Spending?" Issue Update. Washington, DC: The Kaiser Family Foundation.

Hays, Sharon. 1996. *The Cultural Contradictions of Motherhood*. New Haven, CT: Yale University Press.

Hill, Heather, Gretchen Kirby, and Thomas Fraker. 2001. "Delivering Employment Retention and Advancement Services: A Process Study of Iowa's Post-Employment Pilot Program." Report submitted to the Iowa Department of Human Services. Washington, DC: Mathematica Policy Research, Inc. http://www.mathematica-mpr.com/publications/PDFs/iowapep.pdf (accessed October 9, 2008).

Hochschild, Arlie Russell. 1989. *The Second Shift: Working Parents and the Revolution at Home*. New York: Viking.

Holzer, Harry J. 1996. *What Employers Want: Job Prospects for Less-Educated Workers*. New York: Russell Sage Foundation.

Holzer, Harry, and Robert J. LaLonde. 2000. "Job Change and Job Stability among Less-Skilled Young Workers." JCPR Working Paper. Evanston, IL: Joint Center for Poverty Research.

Holzer, Harry, and Karin Martinson. 2005. "Can We Improve Job Retention and Advancement among Low-Income Working Parents?" Working paper. Ann Arbor, MI: National Poverty Center, University of Michigan.

Hulbert, Ann. 2006. "The Time Trap." *New York Times Magazine,* April 2, 6:17.

Johnson, Rucker C., and Mary Corcoran. 2003. "The Road to Economic Self-Sufficiency: Job Quality and Job Transition Patterns after Welfare Reform." *Journal of Policy Analysis and Management* 22(4): 615–639.

Kalil, Ariel, Mary Corcoran, Sandra K. Danziger, Richard Tolman, Kristin Seefeldt, Daniel Rosen, and Yunju Nam. 1998. "Getting Jobs, Keeping Jobs, and Earning a Living Wage: Can Welfare Reform Work?" Institute for Research on Poverty Discussion Paper no. 1170-98. Madison, WI: University of Wisconsin, Madison.

Kennelly, Ivy. 1999. "That Single Mother Element: How White Employers Typify Black Women." *Gender and Society* 13(2): 168–192.

King, Christopher T., and Peter R. Mueser. 2005. *Welfare and Work: Experiences in Six Cities*. Kalamazoo, MI: W.E. Upjohn Institute for Employment Research.

Ku, Leighton. 2005. "Medicaid: Improving Health, Saving Lives." Washington, DC: Center on Budget and Policy Priorities. http://www.cbpp.org/7-19-05health.htm (accessed October 9, 2008).

Levin-Epstein, Jodie. 2006. "Getting Punched: The Job and Family Clock." Policy Brief. Washington, DC: Center for Law and Social Policy.

Levitis, Jason, and Nicholas Johnson. 2006. "Together, State Minimum Wages and State Earned Income Tax Credits Make Work Pay." Washington, DC: Center on Budget and Policy Priorities. http://www.cbpp.org/7-12-06sfp.htm (accessed October 9, 2008).

Loeb, Susanna, and Mary Corcoran. 2001. "Welfare, Work Experience, and Economic Self-Sufficiency." *Journal of Policy Analysis and Management* 20(1):1–20.

Loprest, Pamela. 1992. "Gender Differences in Wage Growth and Job Mobility." *American Economic Review* 82(2): 526–532.

———. 2002. "Disconnected Welfare Leavers Face Serious Risks." Snapshot of America's Families 3, no. 7. Washington, DC: Urban Institute. http://www.urban.org/UploadedPDF/310839_snapshots3_no7.pdf (accessed October 9, 2008).

Mann, Cindy. 1999. "The Ins and Outs of Delinking: Promoting Medicaid Enrollment of Children Who Are Moving In and Out of the TANF System." Report prepared for Covering Kids. Washington, DC: Center on Budget and Policy Priorities.

Marshall, Martin. 1996. "Sampling for Qualitative Research." *Family Practice* 13(6): 522–525.

Mazzeo, Christopher, Brandon Roberts, Christopher Spence, and Julie Strawn. 2006. *Working Together: Aligning State Systems and Policies for Individual and Regional Prosperity.* Brooklyn, NY: Workforce Strategy Center.

Meyer, Bruce, and Douglas Holtz-Eakin. 2001. *Making Work Pay: The Earned Income Tax Credit and Its Impact on American Families.* New York: Russell Sage Foundation.

Michigan Department of Labor and Economic Growth. 2003. "FY 2002 Work First Participant Data." Lansing, MI: Michigan Department of Labor and Economic Growth. http://www.michigan.gov/mdcd/0,1607,7-122-1682-56703--,00.html (accessed October 9, 2008).

Michigan Jobs Commission. 1998. "Work First Monthly Report, November, 1998." Lansing, MI: Michigan Jobs Commission.

Misra, Joya, Stephanie Moller, and Michelle J. Budig. 2007. "Work-Family

Policies and Poverty for Partnered and Single Women in Europe and North America." *Gender and Society* 21(6): 804–827.

Moss, Philip, and Chris Tilly. 2001. *Stories Employers Tell: Race, Skill, and Hiring in America.* New York: Russell Sage Foundation.

Murnane, Richard, and Frank Levy. 1996. *Teaching the New Basic Skills.* New York: The Free Press.

Neal, Derek. 1999. "The Complexity of Job Mobility among Young Men." *Journal of Labor Economics* 17(2): 237–261.

Neckerman, Kathryn M., and Joleen Kirschenman. 1991. "Hiring Strategies, Racial Bias, and Inner-City Workers." *Social Problems* 38(4): 433–447

Neumark, David, Mark Schweitzer, and William Wascher. 2004. "Minimum Wage Effects throughout the Wage Distribution." *Journal of Human Resources* 39(2): 425–450.

Olson, Krista, and LaDonna Pavetti. 1996. "Personal and Family Challenges to the Successful Transition from Welfare to Work: How Prevalent Are These Potential Barriers to Employment?" Report prepared for the Office of the Assistant Secretary for Planning and Evaluation and the Administration for Children and Families. Washington, DC: Urban Institute. http://www.urban.org/publications/406850.html (accessed August 11, 2008).

Pavetti, LaDonna, and Gregory Acs. 1997. "Moving Up, Moving Out, or Going Nowhere? A Study of the Employment Patterns of Young Women." Washington, DC: Urban Institute. http://www.urban.org/publications/406697.html (accessed October 9, 2008).

Payne, Ruby K. 1998. *A Framework for Understanding Poverty.* Highlands, TX: Aha! Process.

Pollack, Harold A., Sheldon Danziger, Kristin S. Seefeldt, and Rukmalie Jayakody. 2002. "Substance Use among Welfare Recipients: Trends and Policy Responses." *Social Service Review* 76(2): 256–274.

Porter, Eduardo. 2006. "Stretched to the Limit, Women Stall March to Work." *New York Times*, March 2, A:1.

Rangarajan, Anu, and Tim Novak. 1999. "The Struggle to Sustain Employment: The Effectiveness of the Postemployment Services Demonstration." Final Report to the Nebraska Department of Health and Human Services. Princeton, NJ: Mathematica Policy Research, Inc.,

Raphael, Jody. 2000. "Domestic Violence as a Welfare-to-Work Barrier: Research and Theoretical Issues." In *Sourcebook on Violence against Women,* Claire Renzetti, J. Edelson, and R. K. Bergen, eds. Thousand Oaks, CA: Sage Publications, pp. 443–456.

Richburg-Hayes, Lashawn. 2008. "Helping Low-Wage Workers Persist in Education Programs." Working Paper. New York: MDRC.

Royalty, Anne Beeson. 1998. "Job-to-Job and Job-to-Nonemployment Turnover by Gender and Education Level." *Journal of Labor Economics* 16(2): 392–443.

Schneider, Greg. 2005. "GM, Ford Bond Ratings Cut to Junk Status." *Washington Post*, May 6, E:01.

Schochet, Peter, and Anu Rangarajan. 2004. "Characteristics of Low-Wage Workers and Their Labor Market Experiences: Evidence from the Mid-to-Late 1990s." Report prepared for the U.S. Department of Health and Human Services. Princeton, NJ: Mathematica Policy Research, Inc.

Scrivener, Susan, and Jenny Au. 2007. "Enhancing Student Services at Lorain County Community College: Early Results from the Opening Doors Demonstration in Ohio." Report to the funders of the Open Doors Project. New York: MDRC.

Seefeldt, Kristin S. 2002. *CQ's Vital Issue Series: Welfare Reform*. Ann C. Lin, series ed. Washington, DC: Congressional Quarterly Press.

Seefeldt, Kristin S., Sheldon Danziger, and Sandra K. Danziger. 2003. "Michigan's Welfare System." In *Michigan at the Millennium: A Benchmark and Analysis of its Fiscal and Economic Structure*, P. Courant, C. Ballard, D. Drake, R. Fisher, and E. Gerber, eds. East Lansing, MI: Michigan State University Press, pp. 351–370.

Seefeldt, Kristin S., Jacob Leos-Urbel, Patricia McMahon, and Kathleen Snyder. 2001. "Recent Changes in Michigan Welfare and Work, Child Care, and Child Welfare Systems." Assessing the New Federalism: State Update No. 4. Washington, DC: Urban Institute. http://www.urban.org/UploadedPDF/MI_update.pdf (accessed October 14, 2008).

Seefeldt, Kristin S., and Sean M. Orzol. 2005. "Watching the Clock Tick: Factors Associated with TANF Accumulation." *Social Work Research* 29(4): 215–229.

Stoll, Michael. 2006. "Job Sprawl, Spatial Mismatch and Black Employment Disadvantage." *Journal of Policy Analysis and Management* 25(4): 827–854.

Story, Louise. 2005. "Many Women at Elite Colleges Set Career Path to Motherhood." *New York Times*, September 20. http://www.nytimes.com/2005/09/20/national/20women.html?scp=3&sq=story%20motherhood&st=cse# (accessed October 9, 2008).

Strawn, Julie, and Victoria Whistler. 2003. "Preliminary Recommendations on Higher Education Act Reauthorization." Comments submitted to the Office of Postscecondary Education, U.S. Department of Education. Washington, DC: The Center for Law and Social Policy. http://www.clasp.org/publications/HEA_comm0203.pdf (accessed October 9, 2008).

Teachman, Jay D., Lucky M. Tedrow, and Kyle D. Crowder. 2000. "The

Changing Demography of America's Families." *Journal of Marriage and the Family* 62(44): 1234–1246.

Thurow, Lester, and Louise Waldstein. 1989. *Toward a High-Wage, High-Productivity Service Sector.* Washington, DC: Economic Policy Institute.

Tolman, Richard M., and Jody Raphael. 2000. "A Review of Research on Welfare and Domestic Violence." *Journal of Social Issues* 56(4): 655–681.

Topel, Robert, and Michael Ward. 1992. "Job Mobility and the Careers of Young Men." *Quarterly Journal of Economics* 107(2): 439–479.

Turner, Lesley J., Sheldon Danziger, and Kristin S. Seefeldt. 2006. "Failing the Transition from Welfare to Work: Women Chronically Disconnected from Employment and Cash Welfare." *Social Science Quarterly* 87(2): 227–249.

U.S. Census Bureau. 2006. "Educational Attainment in the United States, 2006." Washington, DC: U.S. Census Bureau. http://www.census.gov/population/www/socdemo/educ-attn.html (accesssed October 9, 2008).

U.S. Department of Health and Human Services, Administration for Children and Families. 2006. "Marriage Calculator." http://marriagecalculator.acf.hhs.gov/marriage/calculator.php (accessed April 2008).

———. 2008a. "Employment Characteristics of Families in 2007." Washington, DC: U.S. Department of Labor. http://www.bls.gov/news.release/pdf/famee.pdf (accessed April 2008).

———. 2008b. "Local Area Unemployment Statistics." Washington, DC: U.S. Department of Labor. http://www.bls.gov/lau/home.htm (accessed April 2008).

U.S. House of Representatives. 1996. *1996 Overview of Entitlement Programs.* Washington, DC: U.S. Government Printing Office.

Ware, John E., Jr., with Kristin K. Snow, Mark Kosinski, and Barbara Gandek. 1993. *SF-36 Health Survey Manual and Interpretation Guide.* Boston, MA: New England Medical Center, The Health Institute.

Weaver, R. Kent. 2000. *Ending Welfare as We Know It.* Washington, DC: Brookings Institution Press.

Wilson, William J. 1996. *When Work Disappears: The World of the New Urban Poor.* New York: Random House, Inc.

Wood, Robert, and Anu Rangarajan. 2003. "What's Happening to TANF Leavers Who Are Not Employed?" *Mathematica Policy Research Issue Brief* 6(October): 1–4.

Zedlewski, Sheila R. 2003. "Work and Barriers to Work among Welfare Recipients in 2002." Snapshots of America's Families, no. 3. Washington, DC: Urban Institute. http://www.urban.org/UploadedPDF/310836_snapshots3_no3.pdf (accessed October 9, 2008).

The Author

Kristin S. Seefeldt holds a faculty research appointment at the Gerald R. Ford School of Public Policy at the University of Michigan and is the assistant director of the National Poverty Center. She has conducted research and published articles on a variety of social welfare policy issues, including evaluations of welfare-to-work programs as well as analyses of the well-being of former welfare recipients and low-wage workers. Her work has been published in journals such as the *American Journal of Public Health, Social Service Review, Social Science Quarterly*, and the *Annual Review of Sociology*. Currently she is conducting a qualitative study of low-income families' economic coping strategies during economic downturns. She holds a B.A. from Georgetown University, a master's degree in public policy from the University of Michigan, and is completing her doctoral degree at the University of Michigan in sociology and public policy.

Index

The italic letters *f, n,* and *t* following a page number indicate that the subject information of the heading is within a figure, note, or table, respectively, on that page.

About the Institute

The W.E. Upjohn Institute for Employment Research is a nonprofit research organization devoted to finding and promoting solutions to employment-related problems at the national, state, and local levels. It is an activity of the W.E. Upjohn Unemployment Trustee Corporation, which was established in 1932 to administer a fund set aside by Dr. W.E. Upjohn, founder of The Upjohn Company, to seek ways to counteract the loss of employment income during economic downturns.

The Institute is funded largely by income from the W.E. Upjohn Unemployment Trust, supplemented by outside grants, contracts, and sales of publications. Activities of the Institute comprise the following elements: 1) a research program conducted by a resident staff of professional social scientists; 2) a competitive grant program, which expands and complements the internal research program by providing financial support to researchers outside the Institute; 3) a publications program, which provides the major vehicle for disseminating the research of staff and grantees, as well as other selected works in the field; and 4) an Employment Management Services division, which manages most of the publicly funded employment and training programs in the local area.

The broad objectives of the Institute's research, grant, and publication programs are to 1) promote scholarship and experimentation on issues of public and private employment and unemployment policy, and 2) make knowledge and scholarship relevant and useful to policymakers in their pursuit of solutions to employment and unemployment problems.

Current areas of concentration for these programs include causes, consequences, and measures to alleviate unemployment; social insurance and income maintenance programs; compensation; workforce quality; work arrangements; family labor issues; labor-management relations; and regional economic development and local labor markets.

171